# NO MORE MR. NICE GUY

*A Proven Plan for Getting*
*What You Want In Love, Sex, and Life*

## DR. ROBERT A. GLOVER

WITH A NEW FOREWORD BY THE AUTHOR

**SANAGE**
PUBLISHING HOUSE

First published in India by

SANAGE
PUBLISHING HOUSE
Sanage Publishing House

Running Press
Hachette Book Group
1290 Avenue of the Americas, New York, NY 10104
www.runningpress.com
@Running_Press

Printed in the United States

Originally published in paperback and ebook by Barnes & Noble: 2001
First Running Press Edition: January 2003

Published by Running Press, an imprint of Perseus Books, LLC,
a subsidary of Hachette Book Group, Inc.

The Hachette Speakers Bureau provides a wide range of authors for speaking events.
To find out more, go to www.hachettespeakersbureau.com or call (866) 376-6591.

The publisher is not responsible for websites (or their content) that are not
owned by the publisher.

Cover illustration by James Montgomery Flagg
Cover design by Whitney Cookman

Published in arrangement with Barnes & Noble Publishing, Inc.

Library of Congress Control Number: 2002112057

ISBNs: 978-9-3915-6040-9 (paperback)

LSC-C

33  32  31  30  29  28  27  26  25

# DEDICATION
# AND APPRECIATION

No More Mr. Nice Guy *is dedicated to all the men who have so openly and courageously shared their lives and stories with me. This book is about them and for them. Thank you.*

*I also want to express appreciation to all of the people who supported me in writing* No More Mr. Nice Guy. *All the men in my groups and seminars. All the people who read early drafts and gave valuable feedback. Everyone who asked, "Have you finished your book yet?"*

*A special thank you to Elizabeth Oreskovich, Dr. Anne Hastings, Debby Duvall, Nat Sobel, Laura Nolan, and Jennifer Kasius. This book would not exist without your unique contributions.*

# TABLE OF CONTENTS

## NEW PREFACE
## FROM THE AUTHOR

I didn't set out to write a book.

I had begun therapy to work on issues in my marriage. I couldn't figure out why being such a Nice Guy didn't make my wife happy or make her want to have more sex with me. No matter how hard I tried to please her, keep the peace, avoid conflict, and hide my needs, she was still frequently moody, angry, critical, and sexually unavailable. My number-one goal of therapy was to find out why being a Nice Guy didn't make my wife treat me better. Thankfully my early recovery process took me in the healthier direction of learning how to be honest and transparent, set boundaries, live with integrity, love myself, make my needs a priority, express my wants, embrace my passion, and connect with men.

Along the way I began to notice that a number of the men who came to me for therapy were saying many of the things I had thought or said: "Why is she angry all the time?" "It's never enough." "All I want is to be appreciated." "Why doesn't she want to have sex any-more?" "When is it going to be my turn?"

I thought, "Hmmmm, I can finish these guys' sentences for them. They are just like me. I'm not the only guy who thinks that being 'nice' should make people love him, like him, and treat him well."

So I started a bimonthly "No More Mr. Nice Guy" group for a handful of my clients. Every other week I would write a lesson for these men that detailed what I was learning from my exploration of my own Nice Guy issues. I kept writing, and over time the guys—and often their wives and girlfriends—began to tell me, "You should write a book. You should go on *Oprah*."

Well, I never made it onto *Oprah*, but I did end up writing a book.

It took me around six years to write *No More Mr. Nice Guy*. I was not only learning about the Nice Guy Syndrome but also doing my own work and learning how to write, all at the same time. It took another three years to find an agent and secure a publisher.

Countless publishing companies turned down *No More Mr. Nice Guy*, all for the same reason: their marketing departments said men wouldn't buy a self-help book, especially a book that told them they were losers. They all missed the point. The men I wrote about were not only not losers, they were highly motivated to become the best men they could be. Thus, they bought books.

Fortunately, Nat Sobel, an experienced New York literary agent, believed in *NMMNG*. He found the book a publisher, Barnes & Noble, which was launching an eBook publishing venture.

Thanks to a lot of hustle and some very good luck ("Funny how the harder I work, the luckier I get!"), the media picked up on the whole Nice Guy thing, and I enjoyed my fifteen minutes of fame. Barnes & Noble also noticed and partnered with Running Press to publish a print edition of the book in 2003.

Now, almost fifteen years later, sales of *No More Mr. Nice Guy* continues to increase every year. The book has been translated into over a dozen languages. So much for men not buying self-help books!

This reprint offers a good opportunity to share a brief progress report about my personal and professional journey over the fifteen years since the original print edition of *NMMNG* came out. I've said many times, "*No More Mr. Nice Guy* is autobiographical. I just use other guys' stories to tell my own." I've also frequently said, "The book is not a collection of my successes. It is a chronicle of my mistakes."

I didn't write *NMMNG* as some academic sitting in my study, researching the topic of Nice Guys. This book is about my life and the lives of countless Nice Guys with whom I've worked over a significant part of my career. I was the poster child Nice Guy and am now a recovering Nice Guy—I will be until the day I die. At times, like most Nice Guys, I'm "a slow learner and a quick forgetter."

Men seem attracted to *No More Mr. Nice Guy* because it is authentic and honest. I have received thousands of emails from men over the years, asking me how I could know them so well. They tell me how the book has changed their lives and given them direction and hope. It feels good to know that telling the story of my struggles and what I've learned from them has helped so many men (and women) around the world.

When I finished writing *No More Mr. Nice Guy* I had a strong suspicion that I wasn't done with my own journey of discovery and recovery, but I didn't know how right that premonition was.

I was married to my second wife Elizabeth when I started working on my Nice Guy issues and when I wrote this book. She was the big stick upside the head that wouldn't let me wiggle out of addressing my dysfunctional Nice Guy tendencies. I had to go all in and find a different road map for life. Being a Nice Guy just wasn't getting it done.

I will be forever grateful for the force of nature that was Elizabeth in getting me started on my journey. But even as I finished writing *No More Mr. Nice Guy* I knew I wouldn't always need that constant whack upside the head to keep me moving forward. Elizabeth and I separated about six months before the print edition of *NMMNG* came out. I had no way of knowing it at the time, but my life was about to head down a very different road with unseen adventures and a multitude of new growth experiences.

I'll keep the story of my last fifteen years short. I went on my book tour, got divorced, had to learn to live alone for the first time in my adult life, struggled with some depression, frequently felt lost, learned to date in my late 40s, met a lot of great women, had a lot of sex (and couldn't figure out on what planet I had landed after a fourteen-year marriage with virtually no sex), traveled, promoted my book, moved and rebuilt my counseling practice, learned to salsa, worked with thousands more Nice Guys in groups, seminars, online courses, and consultation, started an online university, became a dating coach for men (about which, if you had asked me when I was writing *NMMNG* whether I would ever teach men to date, I would have answered, "No way in hell"), reinvented my business so I could live in Mexico (or anywhere), built a new website, recorded hundreds of podcasts on every aspect of Nice Guy Syndrome recovery, had some great relationships, made some more mistakes, bought a home in Mexico, got married again, became a parent again, am getting better at speaking Spanish (having discovered that marrying a woman who doesn't speak English will do that), signed a contract with Warner Brothers for a television show based on *No More Mr. Nice Guy* (in development as I write this), am working on two more books, and am currently transforming my personal and professional life into being a full-time writer and speaker. Whew!

Personally, I couldn't have predicted fifteen years ago that I would be sitting where I am today. Throughout the years since, my ongoing mantra has been, "I love waking up in the morning not knowing how my day is going to end." I have discovered that when people let go of the inaccurate roadmaps they developed in childhood and begin searching for more helpful life paradigms, they open the door for an amazing adventure.

I also have continued to learn more about myself and about Nice Guys. If I were to add a new chapter to *No More Mr. Nice Guy*, it would be about the effect of anxiety on Nice Guys. In the book I stress the influence of toxic shame but now see that the Nice Guy Syndrome is probably as much about managing anxiety as about managing shame. Learning to self-soothe is every bit as important as learning to release toxic shame.

I say in the book, "Don't try to do this alone," and still believe this as much as ever; this advice will never change. We need the help of safe people to do our work of recovering from the Nice Guy Syndrome.

Fortunately, today the internet, a plethora of books, websites, blogs, forums, programs, retreats, mastermind groups, and coaches focus on helping men do this work. And I am humbled and gratified to hear how many of these resources recommend my book. When I began my recovery process, about all I had to guide me were twelve-step groups and the mythopoetic men's movement led by people like Robert Bly and Michael Meade—"Ho!"

Perhaps you are just beginning your adventure by picking up this edition of *No More Mr. Nice Guy*. Perhaps you have already begun your journey through twelve-step recovery, therapy, or coaching, and you've been recommended this book. Perhaps you've lent your copy of the original edition to a friend, or it is so filled with yellow highlighter that you've decided to pick up the new copy. Wherever you are on your journey, thank you for joining me now. We're going to have a good time.

When I reread my own book in preparation for this new printing, something I had written in the first chapter grabbed my attention:

*"Being integrated means being able to accept all aspects of one's self. An integrated man is able to embrace everything that makes him unique: his power, his assertiveness, his courage, and his passion, as well as his imperfections, his mistakes, and his dark side."*

One thing that has become clearer to me since I finished writing *No More Mr. Nice Guy* almost twenty years ago is this:

*Recovery from the Nice Guy Syndrome is not about becoming a better man or getting rid of anything. Nice Guys have been trying to do both since childhood. Recovery is about becoming more "you."*

You don't have to become a better you to be liked, be loved, get your needs met, or have a good life. You just have to be you. It is actually all the things that you have tried to become or tried to eliminate or hide about you that have gotten in your way all of these years. My profound wish is that this book will help you rediscover, accept, embrace, love–and be–you.

I don't know where life will take me over the next fifteen years. I like that. Perhaps I'll be writing another preface for another edition of *No More Mr. Nice Guy*, and I hope I'll have more changes and discoveries and adventures to write about.

More importantly, I hope this book opens the door for a lifetime of discoveries and adventures as you move in the direction of becoming more you.

Have an adventure. Be you.


Robert Glover
July 2017
Puerto Vallarta, MX

# INTRODUCTION

Five decades of dramatic social change and monumental shifts in the traditional family have created a breed of men who have been conditioned to seek the approval of others.

These men are called *Nice Guys*.

Nice Guys are concerned about looking good and doing it "right." They are happiest when they are making others happy. Nice Guys avoid conflict like the plague and will go to great lengths to avoid upsetting anyone. In general, Nice Guys are peaceful and generous. Nice Guys are especially concerned about pleasing women and being different from other men. In a nutshell, *Nice Guys believe that if they are good, giving, and caring, they will in return be happy, loved, and fulfilled.*

Sound too good to be true?

It is.

Over the last several years, I have encountered countless frustrated and resentful Nice Guys in my practice as a psychotherapist. These men struggle in vain to experience the happiness they so desperately crave and believe they deserve. This frustration is due to the fact that *Nice Guys have believed a myth.*

This myth is the essence of the Nice Guy Syndrome. The Nice Guy Syndrome represents a belief that if Nice Guys are "good," they will be loved, get their needs met, and live a problem-free life. When this life strategy fails to produce the desired results—as it often does—Nice Guys usually just try harder, doing more of the same. Due to the sense of helplessness and resentment this pattern inevitably produces, Nice Guys are often anything but nice.

My exploration of the *Nice Guy Syndrome* grew out of my own frustration of trying to do it "right," yet never getting back what I believed I deserved. I was the typical "sensitive New Age guy"—and proud of it. I believed I was one of the nicest guys you would ever meet. Yet I wasn't happy.

As I began exploring my own Nice Guy behaviors—caretaking, giving to get, fixing, keeping the peace, avoiding conflict, seeking approval, hiding mistakes—I started noticing numerous men with similar traits in my counseling practice. It dawned on me that the script guiding my own life was not an isolated incident, but the product of a social dynamic that affected countless adult males.

Up until now, very few professionals have taken the problem of the Nice Guy Syndrome seriously or offered an effective, comprehensive solution. The earliest reference I have found by a mental health professional to the Nice Guy Syndrome is in a tape recorded in 1985 by Neill Scott, LMSW-ACP. The tape is entitled "The Nice Guy and Why He Always Fails With Women." (See Suggested Resources For Recovering Nice Guys at the end of the book.) Most other references to Nice Guys or the Nice Guy Syndrome address the issue in a humorous manner or from the place of Nice Guys being helpless victims.

This is why I wrote *No More Mr. Nice Guy*.

*This book shows Nice Guys how to stop seeking approval and start getting what they want in love, sex, and life.* The information presented in *No More Mr. Nice Guy* represents a proven plan to help men break free from the ineffective patterns of the Nice Guy Syndrome. It is based on my own experience of recovery, and my work with countless Nice Guys over the last twenty years.

*No More Mr. Nice Guy* is unashamedly pro-male. Nevertheless, countless women have supported the writing of this book. Women who read the book regularly tell me that it not only helps them better understand their Nice Guy partner, it also helps them gain new insights about themselves.

*The information and tools presented in No More Mr. Nice Guy work.* If you are a frustrated Nice Guy, the principles presented in the following pages will change your life. You will:

- Learn effective ways to get your needs met
- Begin to feel more powerful and confident
- Create the kind of intimate relationships you really want
- Learn to express your feelings and emotions
- Have a fulfilling and exciting sex life
- Embrace your masculinity and build meaningful relationships with men
- Live up to your potential and become truly creative and productive
- Accept yourself just as you are

If the above traits sound good to you, your journey of breaking free from the Nice Guy Syndrome has just begun. It is time to stop seeking approval and start getting what you want in love, sex, and life.

# ONE

## THE NICE GUY SYNDROME

**"I'M A NICE GUY. I'M ONE OF THE NICEST GUYS YOU'RE EVER GOING TO MEET."**

Jason, a chiropractor in his midthirties, began his first session of individual therapy with this introduction. Jason described his life as "perfect"—except for one major problem—his sex life. It had been several months since he and his wife Heather had been sexual, and it didn't look like anything was going to change soon.

Jason spoke openly about his marriage, his family, and his sexuality. An affable man, he seemed to welcome the opportunity to talk about himself and his life.

More than anything, Jason wanted to be liked. He saw himself as a very generous, giving person. He prided himself on not having many ups and downs and for never losing his temper. He revealed that he liked to make people happy, and that he hated conflict. To avoid rocking the boat with his wife, he tended to hold back his feelings and tried to do everything "right."

After this introduction, Jason took a piece of paper out of his pocket and began to unfold it. While doing so, he stated that he had written a few things down so he wouldn't forget them.

"I can never do it right," Jason began, looking over his list. "No matter how hard I try, Heather always finds something wrong. I don't deserve to be treated this way. I try to be a good husband and father, but it's never good enough."

Jason paused as he looked over his list.

"This morning is a good example," he continued. "While Heather was getting ready for work, I got our baby Chelsie up, fed her breakfast, and gave her a bath. I had her all ready to go and was about to get ready myself. Then Heather walked in and got that look on her face. I knew I was in trouble."

"'Why'd you dress her in that? That's a good outfit.'" Jason mimicked his wife's tone. "I didn't know she wanted Chelsie to wear something different. After everything I did to get her ready this morning, it was still wrong."

"Here's another example," Jason continued, "the other day I cleaned the kitchen and did a real good job. I loaded the dishwasher, did the pots and pans, and swept the floor. I thought Heather would really appreciate all that I was doing to help out. Before I was finished, she walked in and asked, 'How come you didn't wipe off the counters?' I wasn't even done, for goodness sake. But instead of noticing all that I had done and thanking me, she focused on the one thing I hadn't finished yet."

"Then there is the 'sex thing,'" Jason said. "We only messed around a few times before we got married because we're both Christians. Sex is real important to me, but Heather just isn't interested. I thought once you got married, everything was supposed to be great. After all I do for Heather, you'd think she be willing to give me the one thing I really want."

"I do a lot more than most guys. It seems like I'm always giving so much more than I get." Now, looking like a little boy on the couch, Jason pleaded, "All I want is to be loved and appreciated. Is that too much to ask?"

## Some Of The Nicest Guys You Will Ever Meet

Men like Jason walk into my office on a surprisingly regular basis. These guys come in all shapes and sizes yet they all have the same basic world view. Let me introduce you to a few more.

### Omar

Omar's number one goal in life is to please his girlfriend. Nevertheless, she complains that he is never emotionally available for her. In fact, every one of his previous girlfriends has had the same complaint. Since Omar sees himself as such a giver, he can't understand these accusations. Omar states that his greatest joy in life is making other people happy. He even carries a pager so his friends can get in touch with him if they need anything.

### Todd

Todd prides himself on treating women with honesty and respect. He believes these traits set him apart from other men and should attract women to him. Though he has many female friends, he rarely dates. The women he knows tell him what a great listener he is and often call him to share their problems. He likes feeling needed. These female friends constantly tell him what a great "catch" he will make for some lucky woman. In spite of the way he treats women, he can't understand why they all seem to be attracted to jerks rather than to Nice Guys like him.

### Bill

Bill is the person to whom everyone turns when they need something. The word "no" just isn't in his vocabulary. He fixes cars for women at his church. He coaches his son's little league baseball team. His buddies call on him when they need help moving. He looks after his widowed mother every evening after work. Even though it makes him feel good to give to others, he never seems to get as much as he gives.

## Gary

Gary's wife has frequent rage attacks in which she verbally shames and demeans him. Because he is afraid of conflict and doesn't want to rock the boat, Gary will avoid bringing up subjects that he knows might make his wife angry. After a fight, he is always the first one to apologize. He cannot recall his wife ever saying she was sorry for any of her behaviors. In spite of the constant conflict, Gary says he loves his wife and would do anything to please her.

## Rick

Rick, a gay man in his early forties, is in a committed relationship with an alcoholic. Rick came to counseling to help his partner Jay with his drinking problem. Rick complains that it always feels as if it is up to him to hold everything together. His hope is that if he can help Jay get sober, he will finally have the kind of relationship he has always wanted.

## Lyle

Lyle, a devout Christian, tries to do everything right. He teaches Sunday school and is an elder in his church. Nevertheless, he has struggled since adolescence with an addiction to pornography. Lyle masturbates compulsively, often three to four times a day. He spends hours every day looking at sexually explicit websites on the Internet. He is terrified that if anyone ever finds out the truth about his sexual compulsions, his life will be destroyed. He tries to control his problem with prayer and Bible study, although neither of these approaches has done much good.

### Jose

Jose, a business consultant in his late thirties, has spent the last five years in a relationship with a woman he considers needy and dependent. Jose began thinking about breaking up the day she first moved in. He is afraid that his girlfriend wouldn't be able to make it on her own if he left her. Although he has made several aborted attempts to break up, his girlfriend always becomes such an "emotional basket case" that he gets back together with her. Jose spends just about every waking moment trying to figure out how to get out of the relationship without hurting his girlfriend or looking like a jerk.

## Who Are These Men?

Though all of these men are unique, each shares a common life script: *They all believe that if they are "good" and do everything "right," they will be loved, get their needs met, and have a problem-free life.* This attempt to be good typically involves trying to eliminate or hide certain things about themselves (their mistakes, needs, emotions), and become what they believe others want them to be (generous, helpful, peaceful, etc.).

I call these men *Nice Guys*.

Up to now we haven't paid much attention to the Nice Guy, but he is everywhere.

He is the relative who lets his wife run the show.

He is the buddy who will do anything for anybody, but whose own life seems to be in shambles.

He is the guy who frustrates his wife or girlfriend because he is so afraid of conflict that nothing ever gets resolved.

He is the boss who tells one person what they want to hear, then reverses himself to please someone else.

He is the man who lets people walk all over him because he doesn't want to rock the boat.

He is the dependable guy at church or the club who will never say "no," and would never tell anyone if they were imposing on him.

He is the man whose life seems so under control, until BOOM, one day he does something to destroy it all.

## Characteristics of Nice Guys

Every Nice Guy is unique, but all have a cluster of similar characteristics. These traits are the result of a script, often formed in childhood, that guides their lives. While other men may have one or two of these traits, Nice Guys seem to possess a significant number.

*Nice Guys are givers.* Nice Guys frequently state that it makes them feel good to give to others. These men believe their generosity is a sign of how good they are and will make other people love and appreciate them.

*Nice Guys fix and caretake.* If a person has a problem, has a need, is angry, depressed or sad, Nice Guys will frequently attempt to solve or fix the situation (usually without being asked).

*Nice Guys seek approval from others.* A universal trait of the Nice Guy Syndrome is the seeking of validation from others. Everything a Nice Guy does or says is at some level calculated to gain someone's approval or avoid disapproval. This is especially true in their relationships with women.

*Nice Guys avoid conflict.* Nice Guys seek to keep their world smooth. To do this, they avoid doing things that might rock the boat or upset anyone.

*Nice Guys believe they must hide their perceived flaws and mistakes.* These men are afraid that others will get mad at them, shame them, or leave them if some mistake or shortcoming is exposed.

*Nice Guys seek the "right" way to do things.* Nice Guys believe there is a key to having a happy, problem-free life. They are convinced that if they can only figure out the right way to do everything, nothing should ever go wrong.

*Nice Guys repress their feelings.* Nice Guys tend to analyze rather than feel. They may see feelings as a waste of time and energy. They frequently try to keep their feelings on an even keel.

*Nice Guys often try to be different from their fathers.* Many Nice Guys report having unavailable, absent, passive, angry, philandering, or alcoholic fathers. It is not unusual for these men to make a decision at some point in their lives to try to be 180 degrees different from Dad.

*Nice Guys are often more comfortable relating to women than to men.* Due to their childhood conditioning, many Nice Guys have few male friends. Nice Guys frequently seek the approval of women, and convince themselves they are different from other men. They like to believe that they are not selfish, angry, or abusive—traits they link to "other" men.

*Nice Guys have difficulty making their needs a priority.* These men often feel that it is selfish to put their needs first. They believe it is a virtue to put the needs of others ahead of their own.

*Nice Guys often make their partner their emotional center.* Many Nice Guys report that they are only happy if their partner is happy. Therefore, they will often focus tremendous energy on their intimate relationships.

## What's Wrong With Being A Nice Guy?

We might be tempted to minimize the problem of the Nice Guy Syndrome. After all, how can being nice be such a bad thing? We might even chuckle at the Marvin Milquetoast behaviors of these men as portrayed in comic strips and television sitcoms. Since men already represent an easy target in our culture, the caricature of a sensitive guy might be an object of amusement rather than concern.

Nice Guys themselves frequently have a difficult time grasping the depth and seriousness of their beliefs and behaviors. When I begin working with these men, almost without exception, they all ask, "What is wrong with being a Nice Guy?" Having picked up this book and puzzled over the title, you may be wondering the same thing.

By giving these men the label Nice Guy, I'm not so much referring to their actual behavior, but to their core belief system about themselves and the world around them. These men have been conditioned to believe that if they are "nice," they will be loved, get their needs met, and have a smooth life.

The term Nice Guy is actually a misnomer because Nice Guys are often anything but nice. Here are some not-so-nice traits of Nice Guys:

*Nice Guys are dishonest*. These men hide their mistakes, avoid conflict, say what they think people want to hear, and repress their feelings. These traits make Nice Guys fundamentally dishonest.

*Nice Guys are secretive*. Because they are so driven to seek approval, Nice Guys will hide anything that they believe might upset anyone. The Nice Guy motto is, "If at first you don't succeed, hide the evidence."

*Nice Guys are compartmentalized*. Nice Guys are adept at harmonizing contradictory pieces of information about themselves by separating them into individual compartments in their minds. Therefore, a married man can create his own definition of fidelity which allows him to deny that he had an affair with his secretary (or intern) because he never put his penis in her vagina.

*Nice Guys are manipulative*. Nice Guys tend to have a hard time making their needs a priority and have difficulty asking for what they want in clear and direct ways. This creates a sense of powerlessness. Therefore, they frequently resort to manipulation when trying to get their needs met.

*Nice Guys are controlling*. A major priority for Nice Guys is keeping their world smooth. This creates a constant need to try to control the people and things around them.

*Nice Guys give to get*. Though Nice Guys tend to be generous givers, their giving often has unconscious and unspoken strings attached. They want to be appreciated, they want some kind of reciprocation, they want someone to stop being angry at them, etc. Nice Guys often report feeling frustrated or resentful as a result of giving so much while seemingly getting so little in return.

*Nice Guys are passive-aggressive.* Nice Guys tend to express their frustration and resentment in indirect, roundabout, and not so nice ways. This includes being unavailable, forgetting, being late, not following through, not being able to get an erection, climaxing too quickly, and repeating the same annoying behaviors even when they have promised to never do them again.

*Nice Guys are full of rage.* Though Nice Guys frequently deny ever getting angry, a lifetime of frustration and resentment creates a pressure cooker of repressed rage deep inside these men. This rage tends to erupt at some of the most unexpected and seemingly inappropriate times.

*Nice Guys are addictive.* Addictive behavior serves the purpose of relieving stress, altering moods, or medicating pain. Since Nice Guys tend to keep so much bottled up inside, it has to come out somewhere. One of the most common addictive behaviors for Nice Guys is sexual compulsiveness.

*Nice Guys have difficulty setting boundaries.* Many Nice Guys have a hard time saying "no," "stop," or "I'm not going to." They often feel like helpless victims and see the other person as the cause of the problems they are experiencing.

*Nice Guys are frequently isolated.* Though Nice Guys desire to be liked and loved, their behaviors actually make it difficult for people to get very close to them.

*Nice Guys are often attracted to people and situations that need fixing.* This behavior is often the result of the Nice Guy's childhood conditioning, his need to look good, or his quest for approval. Unfortunately, this tendency pretty much guarantees that Nice Guys will spend most of their time putting out fires and managing crises.

*Nice Guys frequently have problems in intimate relationships.* Though

Nice Guys often put tremendous emphasis on this part of their lives, their intimate relationships are frequently a source of struggle and frustration. For example:

- Nice Guys are often terrible listeners because they are too busy trying to figure out how to defend themselves or fix the other person's problem.
- Because of their fear of conflict, Nice Guys are frequently dishonest and are rarely available to work all the way through a problem.
- It is not unusual for Nice Guys to form relationships with partners whom they believe to be "projects" or "diamonds in the rough." When these projects don't polish up as expected, Nice Guys tend to blame their partner for standing in the way of their happiness.

*Nice Guys have issues with sexuality.* Though most Nice Guys deny having problems with sex, I have yet to meet one who isn't either dissatisfied with his sex life, has a sexual dysfunction (can't get or maintain an erection, climaxes too quickly), or has sexually acted out (through affairs, prostitution, pornography, compulsive masturbation, etc.).

*Nice Guys are usually only relatively successful.* The majority of Nice Guys I've met have been talented, intelligent, and moderately successful. Almost without exception though, they fail to live up to their full potential.

## But He Seemed Like Such A Nice Guy

It is not unusual for unsuspecting people to mistake the passive, pleasing, and generous characteristics of a Nice Guy for those of a healthy male. To many women, the Nice Guy initially appears to be a real catch because the Nice Guy is different from other men they've been with.

Unfortunately, the negative traits listed above find a way to ooze out into Nice Guy's lives and personal relationships. *As a result, these men tend to swing back and forth between being nice and not-so-nice.* I have listened to countless wives, partners and girlfriends describe the Dr. Jekyll and Mr. Hyde qualities of Nice Guys:

"He can be really wonderful and he can also hurt me deeply. He'll do all the extra little things like picking up the kids and fixing dinner when I have to put in extra hours at work. But then out of the blue, he'll throw a tantrum about me never being sexually available to him."

"Everyone thinks he is such a great guy and I'm really lucky to have him. But they don't know what he can really be like. He's always helping people out with their car or something else that needs fixing. When I ask him to do something he tells me that he can never make me happy, and that I'm nagging and controlling like his mother."

"He is constantly trying to please me. He will do anything for me except really be there for me. He'll go shopping with me even though I know he doesn't want to. The whole time he will just sulk, which makes me miserable. I wish he would just tell me 'no' sometimes."

"He will never tell me when something is bothering him. He'll just keep it in and it will build like a pressure cooker. I won't have a clue that anything is bothering him. And then, out of the blue, he'll explode, and we'll end up in a big fight. If he would just tell me when he is upset about something, it would make it a lot easier."

"When I try to talk to him about something that is bothering me, he tries to fix it. He thinks that if I just did everything his way, it would solve all my problems. He always tells me I dwell on the negative and that he can never make me happy. All I really want is for him to listen to me."

"After all the other crummy men I've been with, I thought I had finally found a nice guy that I could trust. Five years into our marriage, I found out that he was addicted to pornography and peep shows. I was devastated. I never even had a clue."

"I wish I could wave a magic wand, keep all of his good traits and make all the others disappear."

## The Integrated Male

After enrolling in a No More Mr. Nice Guy therapy group, Gil, a pleasant man in his early fifties, revealed that his wife was supportive of his joining a group. Nevertheless, he harbored a secret fear that she would be angry at what the name of the group seemed to imply, "How to stop being a Nice Guy and become an S.O.B." Using typical Nice Guy logic, Gil questioned why any woman would be supportive of men becoming "not nice."

Nice Guys tend to be very black and white in their thinking. The only alternative they can see to being nice is becoming "bastards" or "jerks." I frequently remind Nice Guys that the opposite of crazy is still crazy, so becoming a "jerk" isn't the answer.

Recovery from the Nice Guy Syndrome isn't about going from one extreme to another. The process of breaking free from ineffective Nice Guy patterns doesn't involve becoming "not nice." Rather, it means becoming "integrated."

*Being integrated means being able to accept all aspects of one's self.* An integrated man is able to embrace everything that makes him unique: his power, his assertiveness, his courage, and his passion as well as his imperfections, his mistakes, and his dark side.

An integrated male possesses many of the following attributes:

- He has a strong sense of self. He likes himself just as he is.

- He takes responsibility for getting his own needs met.

- He is comfortable with his masculinity and his sexuality.

- He has integrity. He does what is right, not what is expedient.

- He is a leader. He is willing to provide for and protect those he cares about.

- He is clear, direct, and expressive of his feelings.

- He can be nurturing and giving without caretaking or problem-solving.

- He knows how to set boundaries and is not afraid to work through conflict.

An integrated male doesn't strive to be perfect or gain the approval of others. Instead, he accepts himself just as he is, warts and all. An integrated male accepts that he is perfectly imperfect.

Making the transformation from a Nice Guy to an integrated male doesn't come about by just trying harder to be a good man. Breaking free from the Nice Guy Syndrome demands embracing a totally different way of viewing oneself and the world and a complete change in one's personal paradigm. Let me explain.

## Paradigms

A paradigm is the road map we use to navigate life's journey. Everyone uses these road maps, and everyone assumes the map they are using is up-to-date and accurate.

Paradigms often operate at an unconscious level, yet they determine to a large degree our attitudes and behaviors. They serve as a filter through which we process life experiences. Data that does not fit our paradigm is screened out and never reaches our conscious mind. Information that does fit our paradigm is magnified by the process, adding even greater support for that particular way of believing.

Paradigms, like road maps, can be great tools for speeding us along on our journey. Unfortunately, if they are outdated or inaccurate, they can send us in the wrong direction or fruitlessly driving around the same old neighborhood. When this happens we often keep trying harder to find our desired destination while feeling more and more frustrated. Even though an individual following an inaccurate or outdated paradigm may think his behavior makes perfect sense, those around him may wonder what he could possibly be thinking to make him act the way he does.

Most paradigms are developed when we are young, naïve, and relatively powerless. They are often based on the inaccurate interpretations of childhood experiences. Since they are often unconscious, they are rarely evaluated or updated. Unfortunately, these paradigms are assumed to be 100 percent accurate—even when they are not.

## The Ineffective Nice Guy Paradigm

The working paradigm of the Nice Guy is this:

- *If* I can hide my flaws and become what I think others want me to be, *then* I will be loved, get my needs met, and have a problem-free life

Even when this paradigm is ineffective, Nice Guys only see one alternative: *try* harder.

Nice Guys are notoriously slow learners and amazingly quick forgetters when their paradigms are challenged. Their inclination is to hang on to belief systems that have proven to be consistently unworkable, yet are so embedded in their unconscious mind that to challenge them is tantamount to heresy. It is difficult for Nice Guys to consider doing something different, even when what they are doing isn't working.

Jason, whose sexual difficulties with his wife, Heather, were introduced at the beginning of the chapter, is a good example of the frustration that can result from an ineffective Nice Guy paradigm. Jason had a controlling, perfectionist father who put unrealistic demands on Jason and his siblings. His father believed there was one right way to do everything—his way. Jason's mother was an emotionally dependent woman who lived through her children. When his mother was needy, she would smother her kids. When the children had needs, she was often too emotionally distressed to respond.

Jason learned to cope with his childhood experience by developing a paradigm that included:

- Believing that if he could figure out how to do everything right, he could garner his father's approval and avoid his criticism.

- Believing that if he responded to his mother's neediness by being attentive and nurturing, she would be available to him when he had needs.

- Believing that if he was never a moment's problem, he would get love and approval.

- Believing that if he hid his mistakes, no one would ever get mad at him.

As a child, Jason was too naive and powerless to realize that no matter what he did, he would never live up to his father's expectations. Similarly, no matter how giving he was, his needy mother would never be available to nurture him. He could not see that there really was no way to do everything right. And regardless of how well he hid his flaws or mistakes, people might still get angry at him.

Even when his childhood road map failed to take him in the desired direction, the only option he could see was to just keep trying harder doing more of the same. The only thing his paradigm ever really did was to create a distraction from his feelings of fear, worthlessness, and inadequacy.

In adulthood, Jason tried to apply his childhood paradigm to his relationship with his wife. Like his mother, his wife was only attentive when she was emotionally needy. Like his father, she could be critical and controlling. By applying his childhood road map to his marriage—trying to do everything right, being attentive and nurturing, never being a moment's problem, hiding his mistakes—Jason created an illusion that he could get his wife to approve of him all the time, be sexually available whenever he wanted, and never get mad at him. His defective paradigm prevented him from seeing that no matter what he did, his wife would still at times be cold, critical, and unavailable, and that maybe he needed her to be that way. Even when his paradigm was just as ineffective in adulthood as it was in childhood, Jason's only option seemed to be to just keep trying harder.

## Doing Something Different

One of my all-time favorite *Seinfeld* episodes is the one where George decided to change his life by acting the opposite of how he would have typically behaved. Ironically, by doing everything the opposite, he gets a beautiful girlfriend and a job with the Yankees. While doing everything the opposite may not be the answer for breaking free from the Nice Guy Syndrome, doing some things different is.

Over the last several years, I have watched countless men "do something different" by applying the principles contained in this book. These men have transformed themselves from resentful, frustrated, helpless Nice Guys into assertive, empowered, and happy individuals.

Just like George on the *Seinfeld* show, when Nice Guys decide to make a change, interesting things begin to happen. Among other things, I've watched these men:

- Accept themselves just as they are
- Use their mistakes as valuable learning tools
- Stop seeking the approval of others
- Experience loving and intimate relationships
- Make their needs a priority

- Find people who are able and willing to help them meet their needs
- Learn to give judiciously and with no strings attached
- Face their fears
- Develop integrity and honesty
- Set boundaries
- Build meaningful relationships with men
- Create healthier, more satisfying relationships with women
- Experience and express their feelings
- Deal with problems directly
- Develop an intimate and satisfying sexual relationship
- Find peace with the changing complexities of life

## Asking For Help

Nice Guys believe they should be able do everything on their own. They have a difficult time asking for help and try to hide any signs of imperfection or weakness. Breaking free from the Nice Guy Syndrome involves reversing this pattern.

*Recovery from the Nice Guy Syndrome is dependent on revealing one's self and receiving support from safe people. It is essential, therefore, that men who want to break free from the Nice Guy Syndrome find safe people to assist them in this process.*

I encourage recovering Nice Guys to begin this process with a therapist, therapy group, 12-step group, a religious leader, or close friend. Since Nice Guys tend to seek out the approval of women, I strongly encourage them to begin this process with men. For some Nice Guys, the concept of "safe men" may seem like an oxymoron, but I highly recommend it anyway.

I have been leading men's therapy groups for recovering Nice Guys for several years. Some of the most significant aspects of my own recovery from the Nice Guy Syndrome (even before I knew what it was) occurred in the context of 12-step groups and therapy groups. Even though I am sure it is possible to break free from the Nice Guy Syndrome without the help of a group, it is the most effective tool I know for facilitating the recovery process.

## Breaking Free Activities

If you recognize yourself or someone you love in what you have read so far, read on. This book presents a practical and effective guide for breaking free from the negative effects of the Nice Guy Syndrome. This program has worked for countless men and it can work for you or a loved one.

To help facilitate this process, I present numerous Breaking Free activities throughout the book.

These Breaking Free activities serve to facilitate the paradigm shift that is necessary for recovery from the Nice Guy Syndrome. They will not only help recovering Nice Guys understand where their paradigms came from, but will help replace them with more accurate and up-to-date ones. These assignments will also point recovering Nice Guys in a direction that will help them start doing things differently.

### Caution

Before you decide to apply the principles presented in this book, I must first warn you about two things. The first is that the program of recovery presented in *No More Mr. Nice Guy* is not just a few good ideas to try on for size. It represents a challenge to everything Nice Guys believe about what they must do to be loved, get their needs met, and keep their world calm.

*Breaking free from the Nice Guy Syndrome involves a radical change in perspective and behavior. Trying to do it halfway will only result in needless suffering.*

Second, breaking free from the Nice Guy Syndrome will significantly affect your personal relationships. If you are currently in a relationship, I encourage you to ask your partner to read this book along with you. The program of recovery presented in *No More Mr. Nice Guy* will significantly affect you, as well as those closest to you. Though your partner may be supportive of you making positive changes, they may also initially frighten him or her. Reading this book together can help facilitate this transition.

With these warnings aside, if what you have read so far makes sense, keep reading. The following chapters contain information that can help you break free from the Nice Guy Syndrome and start getting what you want in love and life.

---

**BREAKING FREE:**
# ACTIVITY
## 1

Write down three possible safe people or groups that might be able to provide support for you in your recovery from the Nice Guy Syndrome.

If no one comes to mind, get out the telephone directory and look up counselors or support groups in the phone book. Write down three names and phone numbers and call them when you finish this chapter. If you are employed by a company with an Employee Assistance Program, this is another resource. If you know someone who has been to therapy or a support group, ask them for information. If you have access to the Internet you can search for 12-step groups or support groups.

---

**BREAKING FREE:**
# ACTIVITY
## 2

Why would it seem rational for a person to try to eliminate or hide certain things about himself and try to become something different unless there was a compelling reason for him to do so? Why do people try to change who they really are? Take some time and think about this. Is this your behavior or the behavior of someone you know?

---

# TWO

# THE MAKING OF A NICE GUY

I concluded the previous chapter with the questions, "Why would it seem rational for a person to try to eliminate or hide certain things about himself and try to become something different unless there was a compelling reason for him to do so? Why do people try to change who they really are?"

After spending years examining the Nice Guy Syndrome from every possible angle, there is only one answer to this question that makes sense: *because it does not feel safe or acceptable for a boy or man to be just who he is.* Becoming a Nice Guy is a way of coping with situations where it does not feel safe or acceptable for a boy or man to be just who he is. Furthermore, the only thing that would make a child or an adult sacrifice one's self by trying to become something different is a belief that being just who he is must be a bad and/or dangerous thing.

The premise of this book is that during their formative years all Nice Guys received messages from their families and the world around them that it was not safe, acceptable, or desirable for them to be who they were, just as they were.

So how did Nice Guys receive these messages and why did they respond to them in the way that they did? The following is a short course on how families and society turn perfect little boys into men who believe they have to be "good" in order to be loved.

## Coping With Abandonment

The most impressionable time in an individual's life is from birth to about five years. In these first few years a child's personality is most significantly influenced by his surroundings. It is during this time that his paradigms begin to be established. Since the strongest influences during this time are usually a child's parents and extended family, this is where we must begin our examination of the origins of the Nice Guy Syndrome.

There are two important facts we must understand about children. First, when children come into the world they are totally helpless. They are dependent on others to recognize and respond to their needs in a timely, judicious manner. As a result of this dependency, every child's greatest fear is abandonment. To children, abandonment means death.

Second, children are ego-centered. This means that they inherently believe they are the center of the universe and everything revolves around them. Therefore, they believe that they are the cause of everything that happens to them.

These two factors—their fear of abandonment and their ego-centeredness—create a very powerful dynamic for all children. Whenever a child experiences any kind of abandonment he will always believe that he is the cause of what has happened to him. These abandonment experiences might include any of the following:

- He is hungry and no one feeds him
- He cries and no one holds him

- He is lonely and no one pays attention to him
- A parent gets angry at him
- A parent neglects him
- A parent puts unrealistic expectations on him
- A parent uses him to gratify his or her own needs
- A parent shames him
- A parent hits him
- A parent doesn't want him
- A parent leaves him and doesn't come back in a timely manner

Because every child is born into an imperfect world and into an imperfect family, every child has abandonment experiences. Even though their belief that they are the cause of these painful events is, in fact, an inaccurate interpretation of their life, children have no other way to understand the world.

## Toxic Shame

These abandonment experiences and the naive, ego-centered interpretation of them, creates a belief in some young children that it is not acceptable for them to be who they are, just as they are. They conclude that there must be something wrong with them which causes the important people in their lives to abandon them. They have no way of comprehending that their abandonment experiences are not caused by something about them, but by the people who are supposed to recognize and meet their needs.

This naive, ego-centered interpretation of their abandonment experiences creates a psychological state called *toxic shame*. Toxic shame is the belief that one is inherently bad, defective, different, or unlovable. Toxic shame is not just a belief that one does bad things, it is a deeply held core belief that one is bad.

## Survival Mechanisms

As a result of these abandonment experiences and the faulty interpretation of these events, all children develop survival mechanisms to help them do three very important things:

- Try to cope with the emotional and physical distress of being abandoned
- Try to prevent similar events from happening again
- Try to hide their internalized toxic shame (or perceived badness) from themselves and others

Children find a multitude of creative ways to try to accomplish these three goals. Since their insight, experience, and resources are limited, these survival mechanisms are often ineffective and, sometimes, seemingly illogical. For instance, a child who is feeling lonely may misbehave in a way that is sure to attract his parent's attention in a negative way. Even though it may seem illogical for a child to do something that invites painful or negative attention, the consequences of the behavior may not feel as bad as feeling lonely or isolated.

Trying to be "good"–trying to become what he believes others want him to be–is just one of many possible scripts that a little boy might form as the result of childhood abandonment experiences and the internalization of toxic shame.

## The Origin Of The Nice Guy Paradigm

When I first began exploring my own Nice Guy attitudes and behaviors, I had no idea how all the pieces fit together. I believed that I came from a pretty good family and had lived a pretty good life. When I began observing other men with traits similar to my own, I encountered the same general lack of insight into the origins of their own emotional and behavioral patterns.

When questioned about their childhood, Nice Guys frequently

tell me they grew up in "perfect," "great," *Leave It To Beaver*, or "All-American" families. Nevertheless, these men learned to hide their flaws and tried to become what they believed others wanted them to be. These factors indicate that at some point in their early lives, their circumstances were less than ideal.

Alan, Jason, and Jose are all Nice Guys. Each of these men had different childhood experiences. They are all unique in the way that their Nice Guy scripts are played out in their adult lives. In spite of these differences, they all developed a core belief in childhood that they were not OK just as they were. As a result of their internalized toxic shame, each developed a life paradigm that involved seeking approval and hiding perceived flaws. All of these men believed that these life strategies were necessary if they were to have any hope of being loved, getting their needs met, and having a problem-free life.

## Alan

The oldest of three children in a single parent family, Alan prided himself on having never caused his mother a moment's pain. As a child, he performed well in sports and school. He believed that these things set him apart from his siblings and made his mother proud. Alan was the first person in his family to get a college degree, another factor he believed made him special.

Alan's father, an abusive alcoholic, abandoned the family when Alan was seven. At an early age, Alan made a decision to be 180 degrees different from his father. As a result, he prided himself on being patient, giving, and even-keeled. Alan worked hard to never be angry or demeaning like his father. He was an active leader in his youth group at church and never drank alcohol or did drugs as a teenager.

Alan's mother, a fundamentalist Christian, raised Alan in a sect that preached hellfire and brimstone. He came to believe that he was a "sinner" for having normal thoughts, impulses, and behaviors.

Though he always worked hard to be a good Christian, he lived with a constant fear that he might make a mistake and suffer everlasting punishment.

Alan believed his mother was a saint. She would do anything for her children. She would listen and wasn't critical. Frequently, she and Alan would commiserate with each other about all the "bad" things his dad did.

On more than one occasion, Alan's mother told him that she was trying to raise her sons to be different from their father. She wanted them to grow up to be giving, peaceful, and respectful of women. As an adult, Alan still stays in close touch with his mother and does whatever he can to help make her life easier.

### Jason

Jason, introduced in Chapter One, believed he grew up in a *Leave It To Beaver* family. In reality, both of Jason's parents lived through their children. Though he saw his childhood as "ideal," in actuality his parents used him and his siblings to meet their own needs.

Jason believed his parents were "perfect." He described them as being strict and overprotective. He acknowledged that he was sheltered and sexually naive and admitted that he might have been smothered by his parents.

Jason's father closely directed the family. Jason reported that his father still tried to control Jason's life. Jason shared a chiropractic practice with his father, who ran the business, told Jason what house he should buy, what car to drive, and what church he should attend.

Jason described his mother as a "wonderful, loving woman." He reported that she was always involved with the kids. With no friends of her own, she turned to her children for companionship and affirmation of her worth.

Jason couldn't remember his parents showing much affection to each other. He couldn't picture them having sex, and wondered how they made three kids. Even though they did lots of things with the children, he couldn't remember them ever going out or taking a vacation just by themselves.

As an adult, Jason tried to live up to the image of perfection portrayed by his parents. Everything he did was calculated to look good: he looked like a good husband, a good father, a good Christian, and a good professional. In spite of all his efforts, he always felt inadequate and defective compared to his parents.

### Jose

A successful business consultant, Jose was afraid of intimate relationships. Jose was highly educated and had a stressful, high-powered career. He was physically active, and his idea of recreation was taking a hundred-mile bike ride or climbing a mountain. He repressed his anger and tried to never say anything that would upset anyone. He saw himself as controlling, and acknowledged that his drug of choice was "recognition."

Jose was attracted to dependent women. He found it interesting that he seemed to be attracted to incest survivors. He stayed in his present relationship because he was concerned about the financial welfare of his girlfriend. He was afraid she wouldn't make it if he left.

Jose openly acknowledged that he came from a dysfunctional family. He was the second of seven children in a working class family. At around the age of 14, he took on the role of parenting his younger siblings. Jose reported that there was tremendous chaos in his family, and he saw his job as protecting his brothers and sisters from its effects.

Jose saw his father as angry, controlling, and abusive. He was explosive and demeaning to the boys and sexually abusive to the girls.

Jose's mother was manic-depressive. She had extreme mood swings and had a difficult time staying on her medication. When she was manic, the house would be spotless, she would talk of entertaining politicians and socialites, and she would begin destructive sexual relationships. When she was depressed, she kept the windows covered, the house became a wreck, and she would threaten to kill herself. When he was 15, Jose had to break through a locked door and take a loaded gun away from his mother. She had been threatening suicide while all seven kids stood by terrified. Jose saw this as a typical scenario growing up in his home.

Jose worked hard all of his life to be different from his family. His family had him on a pedestal, and he was the one to whom everyone turned whenever they had a problem. His job as a family member was fixing chaos. His job as a business consultant was fixing chaos. His role in relationships was fixing chaos. Jose's life script required chaos because without it he would be out of a job.

Jose considered his natural intelligence, work ethic, and ability to solve problems his "saving grace." He believed these factors allowed him to escape his family dysfunction and make something of himself. Without them, he was convinced, he would have ended up just like his parents and the rest of his siblings.

## Child Development 101

Alan, Jason, and Jose all had very different childhood experiences, yet all developed a similar script that guided their lives. Each, in various ways, internalized a belief that they were not OK just as they were, and their survival depended on becoming something different. To help us connect the dots and see how three very different childhood experiences could create three men with very similar life paradigms, it might be helpful to do a quick review of the child development principles presented earlier in this chapter:

- All children are born totally helpless.
- A child's greatest fear is abandonment.

- All children are ego-centered.
- All children have numerous abandonment experiences when their needs are not met in a timely, judicious manner.
- When a child has an abandonment experience, he always believes that he is the cause.
- This naive misinterpretation creates toxic shame–a belief that he is "bad."
- Children develop survival mechanisms to cope with their abandonment experiences, to prevent the experiences from happening again, and to hide their "badness" from themselves and others.
- These childhood survival mechanisms reflect the child's inherent powerlessness and naive view of himself and the world.

## From Perfect Little Boys To Nice Guys

The principles above can be applied to the childhood experiences of Alan, Jason, Jose, and every other Nice Guy described in this book. The progression from perfect little boy to Nice Guy basically occurs in three stages: abandonment, internalization of toxic shame, and the creation of survival mechanisms.

### Abandonment

Like all Nice Guys, Alan, Jason, and Jose were abandoned in various ways.

Alan and Jose had an angry or critical parent who communicated that they were not OK just as they were.

Alan worshipped his mother, but she would not intervene when his father lashed out at Alan. This implied that he wasn't worth protecting.

Alan came to believe that he had to be different from his father to be seen as a good man and be loved by his mother.

Alan and Jason were used and objectified by their parents. They were valued for always doing it "right" and never being a problem. This communicated that they were only lovable when they lived up to their parents' expectations.

Since Jason believed his parents were "perfect," he always felt flawed and inadequate compared to them.

Neither of Jose's parents provided any guidance, nurturing, or support. This communicated that he was of little or no value to them.

Alan and Jason grew up in fundamentalist churches that reinforced a need to be perfect and sinless. Failure to do so meant everlasting punishment.

Jose believed he was valuable only if he was different from his crazy family.

All three—Alan, Jason, and Jose—believed that someone else's needs were more important than their own—a common occurrence in Nice Guy families.

All of these experiences represented a form of abandonment because they communicated to these little boys that they were not OK just as they were.

### Shame

Regardless of whether they were abused, abandoned, neglected, shamed, used, smothered, controlled, or objectified, all Nice Guys internalized the same belief—*it was a bad or dangerous thing for them to be just who they were.*

Some of these messages were communicated overtly by parents who had no concern for the child's welfare. Some were communicated indirectly by caring parents who themselves were too young, overwhelmed, or distracted to provide a nurturing environment for their child. At times, these messages were communicated by circumstances that were beyond anyone's control.

In every situation, the child believed these events and circumstances were telling a story about him. He believed there was something about him that caused these things to happen. Using child-like logic he concluded, "*There must be something wrong with me because––.*" Fill in the blank:

- When I cry, no one comes.
- Mom gets that look on her face.
- Dad left and didn't come back.
- Mom has to do everything for me.
- Dad yells at me.
- I'm not perfect like Mom and Dad.
- I can't make Mom happy.

These childhood experiences also caused the young boy to believe, "*I'm only good enough and lovable when–.*" Fill in the blank:

- I'm different from Dad.
- Mom needs me.
- I don't make any mistakes.
- I make good grades.
- I'm happy.
- I'm not like my brother.
- I don't cause anyone any problems.
- I make Mom and Dad happy.

### Survival Mechanisms

As a result of their childhood abandonment experiences and the inaccurate interpretation of these events, all Nice Guys develop survival mechanisms to help them do three very important things:

- Try to cope with the pain and terror caused by their abandonment experiences

- Try to prevent these abandonment experiences from occurring again
- Try to hide their toxic shame from themselves and others

For Nice Guys, these survival mechanisms take the form of the following life paradigm:

- *If* I can hide my flaws and become what I think others want me to be, *then* I will be loved, get my needs met, and have a problem-free life

It is this paradigm, formed in childhood, that guides and controls everything Nice Guys do in their adult lives. Even though it is based on faulty interpretations of childhood events, it is the only road map these men have. Nice Guys believe this map is accurate, and if they follow it correctly they should arrive at their desired location: a smooth, happy life. Even though this life script is often highly ineffective, Nice Guys frequently just keep trying harder, doing more of the same, hoping for different results.

## Two Kinds Of Nice Guys

The survival mechanisms that Nice Guys develop to deal with their abandonment experiences and internalized toxic shame are usually manifested in one of two ways. In one form, a Nice Guy exaggerates his toxic shame and believes he is the worst kind of person. I call this man the "I'm so bad" Nice Guy.

The "I'm so bad" Nice Guy is convinced everyone can see how bad he is. He can give concrete examples of bad behavior in childhood, adolescence, and adulthood that support his core belief about himself. He can tell of breaking windows and getting whippings as a little boy. He will reveal running afoul of the law and making his mother cry when he was a teenager. He will tell tales of smoking, drinking, using drugs and carousing as an adult. He is convinced his only hope for having any kind of happiness in life lies in trying his best to mask his inherent badness. He never really believes anyone will buy into his Nice Guy persona, but doesn't think he has any other choice.

The second kind of Nice Guy is the "I'm so good" Nice Guy. This man handles his toxic shame by repressing his core belief about his worthlessness. He believes he is one of the nicest guys you will ever meet. If he is conscious of any perceived flaws, they are seen as minor and easily correctable. As a child he was never a moment's problem. As a teen he did everything right. As an adult, he follows all the rules to a tee. This Nice Guy has tucked his core toxic shame into a handy, air-tight compartment deep in his unconscious mind. He masks his toxic shame with a belief that all the good things he does make him a good person.

Even though the two kinds of Nice Guys may differ in their conscious awareness of their toxic shame, both operate from the same life paradigm. All Nice Guys believe they are not OK just as they are, and therefore must hide their flaws and become what they believe other people want them to be.

I make the distinction between the two kinds of Nice Guys to help both see their distortions. Neither is as bad or good as they believe themselves to be. They are both just wounded souls operating from a belief system based on the inaccurate perceptions of the events of their childhood.

---

**BREAKING FREE:**
# ACTIVITY
## 3

It is impossible to cover every factor that might cause a young boy to try to hide his perceived flaws and seek approval from others. I don't believe it is essential for Nice Guys to uncover every experience that ever made them feel unsafe or bad. But I have found that some understanding of where a life script originated is helpful in changing that script.

Reread the stories of Alan, Jason, and Jose. Think about how these stories are similar to your own childhood experiences. On a separate piece of paper or in a journal, write down or illustrate the messages you received in your family that seemed to imply that it wasn't OK for you to be who you were, just as you were. Share these experiences with a safe person. As you do, note your feelings. Do you feel sad, angry, lonely, numb? Share this information as well.

The purpose of this assignment is to name rather than blame. Blaming will keep you stuck. Naming these childhood experiences will allow you to replace these messages with more accurate ones and help you change your Nice Guy script.

---

## The Baby Boom Generation And The Sensitive Guy

Every child who has ever lived has experienced various forms of abandonment. There are many ways in which children can interpret and respond to these events. As stated above, becoming a Nice Guy is just one of many possible reactions. The childhood experiences described above are probably not sufficient in themselves, however, to account for the multitude of Nice Guys I encounter regularly.

I have no doubt that Nice Guys have always existed. There have always been Marvin Milquetoast and Walter Mitty kinds of guys out there. I'm sure there has never been a shortage of mama's boys and henpecked husbands. I believe many little boys are born with a peaceful, generous temperament and grow up to be peaceful, generous men. But after years of working with countless men, I am convinced that a unique combination of social dynamics over the last five decades has produced a plethora of Nice Guys in historically unprecedented numbers.

To truly understand the current phenomena of the Nice Guy Syndrome, we have to take into account a series of significant social changes that began around the turn of the century and accelerated following World War II. These social dynamics included:

- The transition from an agrarian to an industrial economy
- The movement of families from rural areas to urban areas
- The absence of fathers from the home
- The increase in divorce, single parent homes, and homes headed by women.
- An educational system dominated by women
- Women's liberation and feminism
- The Vietnam War
- The sexual revolution

These events combined to have a major impact on American boys growing up in this era. These social changes created three profound dynamics that contributed to the widespread phenomena of the Nice Guy Syndrome in the baby boom generation.

*Boys were separated from their fathers and other significant male role models.* As a result, men became disconnected from other men in general and confused as to what it meant to be male.

*Boys were left to be raised by women.* The job of turning boys into men was left to mothers and a school system dominated by women. As a result, men became comfortable being defined by women and became dependent on the approval of women.

*Radical feminism implied that men were bad and/or unnecessary.* The messages of radical feminism furthered the belief of many men that if they wanted to be loved and get their needs met, they had to become what they believed women wanted them to be. For many men, this meant trying to hide any traits that might cause them to be labeled as "bad" men.

# Twentieth Century History 101

The following is a brief overview of how some of the dynamic social changes of the last half of the twentieth century helped create the bumper crop of Nice Guys in our culture.

## The Loss Of Fathers

The shift to a manufacturing society and urban migration in the post-war years took fathers away from their sons in droves. According to the U.S. census, in 1910 one third of all families lived on farms. By 1940, this number had shrunk to one in five. By 1970, 96 percent of all families lived in urban areas.

In an agrarian society, boys connected with their fathers by working alongside them in the fields. This often meant contact with extended family that included grandfathers, uncles, and cousins. This daily contact with men provided boys with an intimate model of maleness. Sons learned about being male by watching their dads, just as their own fathers had learned by watching their fathers. As families migrated from rural areas to cities and suburbs after World War II, the contact between fathers and sons diminished significantly. Dads left home in the morning and went to work. Most sons never got to see what their fathers did, let alone have much time to spend with them.

Fathers became unavailable in other ways. Men's addictions to work, TV, alcohol, and sex took them away from their sons. Increases in divorce began to separate boys from their fathers. Census statistics show that the incidence of divorce tripled from 1940 to 1970. In 1940, just over five million households were headed by women. By 1970, this figure had almost tripled to over 13 million households.

In general, the Nice Guys I have worked with do not report having had a close, bonded relationship with their fathers in childhood. Sometimes this was a result of their fathers working long hours, being withdrawn, or being passive. More often than not, Nice Guys describe their fathers in negative terms. They often see them as controlling, rageful, angry, absent, abusive, unavailable, addictive, or philandering. It is not unusual at some point in childhood for Nice Guys to have made a conscious decision to be different from their fathers.

The unavailability of dads during this era often required mothers to take over the job of the fathers. Women inherited the defacto job of turning boys into men. Unfortunately, even the most well-meaning mothers are not equipped to teach their sons how to be men by themselves. This hasn't kept them from trying.

I believe the significant number of Nice Guys produced in the '40s, '50s, and '60s is the direct result of mothers, not fathers, teaching their sons how to be male. Consequently, many Nice Guys have adopted a female perspective of masculinity and are comfortable having their manhood defined by women.

### The Female Dominated
### Educational System

The modern educational system has also contributed to the dynamic of boys being raised by women. Since World War II, boys have entered schools dominated by females. For most boys, the first several years in school become basic training in how to please women. From kindergarten through sixth grade, I had only one male teacher and six female teachers. This is pretty consistent with national norms.

Men account for just one in four teachers nationwide. In the primary grades, they make up only 15 percent of the teaching staff, and that number is steadily dropping. From daycare to preschool to elementary school, little boys in the postwar era have been surrounded by women. There have been few adult males to help them through this experience. If a little boy was already disconnected from his father and trained to please a woman, the typical school system magnified this conditioning.

## The Vietnam War

In the '60s, the Vietnam War crystallized the feeling of alienation between many baby-boom boys and their fathers. Battle lines were drawn between young men protesting a war started and perpetuated by their fathers. A generation of World War II veterans could not understand the flaunting of responsibility and the social rebellion of their sons. The young men of this generation became the antithesis of their fathers and of an establishment that solved domestic and international problems with guns and bombs. The antiwar movement created a new breed of males focused on love, peace, and avoiding conflict.

## Women's Liberation

During this same period of time, many women were beginning to work outside of the home, birth control provided new freedom, and women's liberation was in its infancy. Some mothers during the Baby Boom era could foresee a change in gender roles on the horizon. They worked to prepare their sons and daughters for what was to come. Many of these mothers raised their daughters to not need a man. At the same time, they trained their sons to be different from their fathers—peaceful, giving, nurturing, and attentive to a woman's needs.

Radical feminism in the '60s and '70s projected an angry generalization about men. Some feminists claimed that men were the cause of all of the problems in the world. Others asserted that men were merely an unnecessary nuisance. More than likely, the majority of women during this era did not feel this way about men. Nevertheless, enough angry women were significantly vocal to contribute to a social climate that convinced many men that it was not OK to be just who they were.

Epithets like "men are pigs" and "all men are rapists" were prominent during this time. Less angry slogans of feminism asserted that "a woman needs a man like a fish needs a bicycle." Men who were already conditioned to look to women for definition and approval were especially susceptible to these kinds of messages. This added incentive for these men to try to figure out what women wanted and to try to become that in order to be loved and get their needs met.

## Soft Males And Boy-Men

Robert Bly, the author of *Iron John*, writes about how the social changes of the Baby Boom era created a new breed of American men. Bly calls these men "soft males."

He writes, "They're lovely, valuable people—I like them—they're not interested in harming the earth or starting wars. There's a gentle attitude toward life in their whole being and style of living. But many of these men are not happy. You quickly notice the lack of energy in them. They are life-preserving but not exactly life-giving. Ironically, you often see these men with strong women who positively radiate energy. Here we have a finely-tuned young man, ecologically superior to his father, sympathetic to the whole harmony of the universe, yet he himself has little vitality to offer."

From a different perspective, Camille Paglia comments on how the social changes of the last five decades have changed the roles of men and women. "The hard-driving woman has to switch personae (sic) when she gets home. She's got to throttle back, or she'll castrate everything in the domestic niche. Many white, middle-class women have dodged this dilemma by finding themselves a nice, malleable boy-man who becomes another son in the subliminally matriarchal household." ("Politically Incorrect Desires," Salon: Issue 49)

Regardless of whether we call these men "soft males," "sensitive New Age guys," or "Nice Guys," the unique combination of social events in the post-World War II era reinforced and magnified the messages that many little boys had already received from their families—that they weren't OK just as they were. These social events further amplified the belief that if they wanted to be loved, get their needs met, and have a smooth life, they had to hide their flaws and become what others (especially women) wanted them to be.

My observation in recent years points to the reality that the conditioning described above did not end with the Baby Boom generation. I am seeing more and more young men in their twenties, and even teens, who demonstrate all of the characteristics of the Nice Guy Syndrome. Not only have these young men have been affected by all of the social dynamics listed above, even more grew up in single parent families or were raised by Nice Guy fathers. As I write this, I expect that we are just beginning on our third generation of Nice Guys.

## The Habits Of Highly Ineffective Men

As a result of the family and social conditioning described above, Nice Guys struggle to get what they want in love and life. Due to their shame and ineffective survival mechanisms, the road map they follow just won't take them where they want to go. This is frustrating. But rather than trying something different, their life paradigm requires that they keep trying harder, doing more of the same.

I frequently tell Nice Guys, "If you keep doing what you've always done, you'll keep getting what you've always had." To reiterate what I've illustrated before, Nice Guys prevent themselves from getting what they want in love and life by:

- Seeking the approval of others
- Trying to hide their perceived flaws and mistakes
- Putting other people's needs and wants before their own
- Sacrificing their personal power and playing the role of a victim
- Disassociating themselves from other men and their own masculine energy

- Co-creating relationships that are less than satisfying
- Creating situations in which they do not have very much good sex
- Failing to live up to their full potential

The next seven chapters present a proven plan to show recovering Nice Guys the most effective ways to do something different. Read on. It is time for you to start getting what you want in love and life.

# chapter THREE

## LEARN TO PLEASE YOURSELF

"I'm a chameleon," revealed Todd, a 30-year-old single Nice Guy. "I will become whatever I believe a person wants me to be in order to be liked. With my smart friends I act intelligent and use a big vocabulary. Around my mother, I look like the perfect loving son. With my dad, I talk sports. With the guys at work I cuss and swear…whatever it takes to look cool. Underneath it all, I'm not sure who I really am or if any of them would like me just for who I am. If I can't figure out what people want me to be, I'm afraid I will be all alone. The funny thing is, I feel alone most of the time anyway."

Just about everything a Nice Guy does is consciously or unconsciously calculated to gain someone's approval or to avoid disapproval. Nice Guys seek this external validation in just about every relationship and social situation, even from strangers and people they don't like. Todd is an example of a man who, because of internalized toxic shame, believes he has to become what he thinks other people want him to be.

The seeking of external validation is just one way in which

Nice Guys frequently do the opposite of what works. By trying to please everyone, Nice Guys often end up pleasing no one—including themselves.

## Seeking Approval

Because Nice Guys do not believe they are OK just as they are, they find a multitude of ways to convince themselves and others that they are lovable and desirable. They may focus on something about themselves (physical appearance, talent, intellect), something they do (act nice, dance well, work hard), or even something external to themselves (attractive wife, cute child, nice car) in order to get value and win other's approval.

My word for these value-seeking mechanisms is attachments. Nice Guys attach their identity and worth to these things and use them to convince themselves and others that they are valuable. Without these attachments, Nice Guys don't know what else about themselves would make anyone like or love them. Being a Nice Guy is the ultimate attachment for these men. They genuinely believe their commitment to being "good" and doing it "right" is what makes them valuable and compensates for their internalized belief that they are bad.

Because of their toxic shame, it is impossible for Nice Guys to grasp that people might like them and love them just for who they are. They believe they are bad (the "I'm So Good" Nice Guy is unconscious of this core belief, but it is a core belief nonetheless), and therefore they assume that if anyone really got to know them, they would discover the same thing. Being able to attach themselves to things that make them feel valuable and garner approval from others seems essential if they hope to be loved, get their needs met, and have a problem free life.

# ACTIVITY

**4**

I've taken surveys in several No More Mr. Nice Guy groups asking the members about the attachments they use to try to get external approval. The following are just a few of the responses. Look over the list. Note any of the ways in which you seek approval. Add to the list any behaviors that are uniquely you. Write down examples of each. Ask others for feedback about the ways in which they see you seeking approval.

- Having one's hair just right
- Being smart
- Having a pleasant, non-threatening voice
- Appearing unselfish
- Being different from other men
- Staying sober
- Being in good shape
- Being a great dancer
- Being a good lover
- Never getting angry
- Making other people happy
- Being a good worker
- Having a clean car
- Dressing well
- Being nice
- Respecting women
- Never offending anyone
- Appearing to be a good

## How Nice Guys Use Attachments

Cal is a typical Nice Guy in the way he uses attachments to seek approval. Cal tries to get external validation by always being in a good mood, driving a nice car, dressing well, having a cute daughter, and having an attractive wife. Let's pick one of these attachments to illustrate how Cal tries to get approval from others.

Cal likes to dress his 14-month-old daughter in a cute dress and take her to the park. From the moment he begins to dress her, he is unconsciously attaching his value and identity to the acknowledgment he thinks he will receive from being a "good dad." He knows that when he takes his daughter walking people will look at her and smile. Some will comment about the cute little girl and her father out for a walk. A few will stop and ask her age, and others will gush about what a precious little angel she is. This attention makes Cal feel good about himself.

The irony is that no one really values Cal for his attachments. Further, his dependency on external validation actually prevents people from getting to know him just as he is. None of these things have anything to do with who he is as a person. Nevertheless, they are the things he believes give him identity and value.

## Seeking The Approval Of Women

Nice Guys seek external validation in just about every social situation, but their quest for approval is the most pronounced in their relationships with women. Nice Guys interpret a woman's approval as the ultimate validation of their worth. Signs of a woman's approval can take the form of her desire to have sex, flirtatious behavior, a smile, a touch, or attentiveness. At the other end of the spectrum, if a woman is depressed, in a bad mood, or angry, Nice Guys interpret these things to mean that she is not accepting or approving of them.

There are numerous negative consequences in seeking the approval of women.

*Seeking a woman's approval requires Nice Guys to constantly monitor the possibility of a woman's availability.* The *possibility of availability* is a term I use to describe the subjective measure of a woman's sexual availability. Since Nice Guys see sex as the ultimate form of acceptance, and they believe a woman must be in a good mood before she will have sex, these men are constantly diligent to not do anything that might upset a woman whom they desire. In addition, if a woman they desire is angry, depressed, or in a bad mood, they believe they must do something quickly—lie, offer solutions, sacrifice self, manipulate—to fix it.

The possibility of availability extends beyond just sex. Since Nice Guys have been conditioned by their families and society to never do anything to upset a woman, they are hyper vigilant in responding to the moods and desires of women they don't even plan on having sex with.

*Seeking women's approval gives women the power to set the tone of the relationship.* Nice Guys constantly report that their own moods are often tied to the moods of their partner. If she is happy and doing OK, so is he. If she is angry, depressed, or stressed, he will feel anxious until she feels better. This connection runs so deep that many Nice Guys have told me that they feel guilty if they are in a good mood when their partner is not.

*Seeking women's approval gives women the power to define men and determine their worth.* If a woman says he is "wrong" or thinks he is a "jerk," a Nice Guy will be inclined to believe she is right. Even if the Nice Guy argues with the woman's evaluation, at some level he knows that, since she is the woman, she must be right. (One Nice Guy asked me, "If a man is talking in the forest and no woman is there to hear him, is he still wrong?")

*Seeking women's approval creates rage toward women.* Though most Nice Guys claim to "love" women, the truth is most of these men have tremendous rage toward women. This is because we tend to eventually despise whatever we make into our god. When our god fails to respond in the ways we expect, we humans tend to respond in one of two ways. We either blindly intensify our acts of worship or lash out in righteous anger. When Nice Guys put a woman or women on a pedestal and attempt to win their approval, sooner or later, this adoration will turn to rage when these objects of worship fail to live up to the Nice Guys' expectations. This is why it is not unusual to hear a Nice Guy proclaim his undying love to a woman in one breath and then ragefully call her a "f...c..." only moments later.

I have found that many gay Nice Guys are just as susceptible as straight men to seeking women's approval. As long as the gay Nice Guy can convince himself that he is not sexually attracted to women, he can delude himself into thinking that women don't have any power over him.

---

**BREAKING FREE:**
# ACTIVITY
## 5

Consider this:

If you did not care what people thought of you, how would you live your life differently?

If you were not concerned with getting the approval of women, how would your relationships with the opposite sex be different?

---

## Cover-Up Artists

When my son Steve was nine years old, he accidentally poked some holes in our kitchen table with a ballpoint pen. When he realized what he had done, he immediately showed his mother the damage. Steve had appropriate, healthy shame about his mistake. He knew that his actions had caused damage to the table. He also knew that he had to take responsibility. Most importantly, he knew he wasn't bad.

If I had done the same thing as a child (or even as an adult), I would have had an attack of toxic shame and tried my best to hide or deny what I had done. I would have been convinced someone was going to be angry at me and stop loving me. I would have lived with the secret, as well as with a constant fear of being found out.

Numerous Nice Guys have commented that they could relate to my son's situation. Without exception, every one of them has admitted that they would have done the opposite of what Steve did—tried to cover it up.

As stated above, everything a Nice Guy does is calculated to try to win approval or avoid disapproval. Since Nice Guys do not believe they are OK just as they are, they see any mistake or perceived flaw as proof that they are bad and unlovable. They believe that if anyone sees how bad they really are, they will be hurt, shamed, or abandoned. As a result, Nice Guys are consummate cover-up artists.

Nice Guys believe they must hide or distract attention from any perceived shortcoming:

- If they forget something
- If they are late
- If they break something
- If they don't understand something
- If they do something wrong
- If they are depressed
- If they are in pain
- If they generally mess up

The Nice Guy's need to hide is often the most pronounced in areas that are just part of being human and alive.

- That they are sexual
- That they have bodily functions
- That they are getting older
- That they are losing their hair
- That they have needs
- That they are imperfect

Look over the lists above. Write down examples of situations in which you have tried to hide or distract attention from any of these perceived flaws. How effective do you think you are in keeping these things hidden from the people you love?

## Hiding The Evidence

Nice Guys find many creative ways to cover up their perceived flaws and mistakes. These include:

### Lying

Most Nice Guys pride themselves on being honest and trustworthy. Ironically, Nice Guys are fundamentally dishonest. Nice Guys will tell lies, partial truths, and omit information if they believe it will prevent someone from focusing on them in a negative way.

### Drawing On Their Account

Since Nice Guys strive so hard to be good, giving, and caring, they believe these acts should build up a credit that wipes clean any wrong they might do. Part of the Nice Guy's belief is that if he does most things right, no one should ever notice the few things (if any) he does wrong.

### Fixing

Mature people take responsibility for their actions. When they make a mistake or act inappropriately, they apologize, make amends, or repair the damage. Conversely, Nice Guys try to fix situations by doing whatever it takes to get the other person to stop being upset.

### DEER Response

DEER is an acronym I use for: Defend, Explain, Excuse, Rationalize. These are all fear-based behaviors used to distract others from focusing on the Nice Guy's mistakes and "badness." The Nice Guy is most likely to go into the DEER Response when he has done something or failed to do something, and someone (usually wife, partner, or boss) confronts him and expresses his or her feelings.

### Turning The Tables

If someone gets angry at a Nice Guy or points out some flaw or mistake, his shame will be triggered. In an attempt to distract himself and the other person from his "badness" he may try to turn the tables and do something to trigger the other person's shame. I call this *shame dumping*. This unconscious strategy is based on the belief that if the Nice Guy can shift the focus to the other person's badness, he can slip out of the spotlight. Typical shame dumping techniques include blame, bringing up the past, deflection, and pointing out the other person's flaws.

### Walls

Nice Guys build walls that prevent others from getting too close. Understandably, this affects their ability to be intimate, but it also protects them from the consequences of being found out. These walls might include: addictions (food, sex, T.V., alcohol, work, etc.), humor, sarcasm, intellectualism, perfectionism, and isolation.

## Teflon Men

As much as Nice Guys try to look good and get people to like them, the above defenses keep people at arm's length. Like most Nice Guy patterns, these unconscious behaviors actually accomplish the exact opposite of what the Nice Guy really craves. While desiring love and connection, his behaviors serve as an invisible force field that keeps people from being able to get close to him.

Nice Guys have a difficult time comprehending that in general, people are not drawn to perfection in others. People are drawn to shared interests, shared problems, and an individual's life energy.

Humans connect with humans. Hiding one's humanity and trying to project an image of perfection makes a person vague, slippery, lifeless, and uninteresting. I often refer to Nice Guys as *Teflon Men*. They work so hard to be smooth, nothing can stick to them. Unfortunately, this Teflon coating also makes it difficult for people to get close. It is actually a person's rough edges and human imperfections that give others something to connect with.

## Self-Approval

Recovery from the Nice Guy Syndrome involves changing core paradigms. Instead of seeking external validation and avoiding disapproval, recovering Nice Guys must begin seeking their own approval.

Ironically, when Nice Guys begin focusing on pleasing themselves, they actually begin to experience the intimacy and connection with others that they have always desperately craved. To help facilitate this recovery process, Nice Guys can:

- Identify how they seek approval
- Take good care of themselves
- Give themselves positive affirmations
- Spend extended periods of time alone
- Reveal themselves to safe people

Consider these questions:

Do you believe that people can see your human imperfections and still love you?

How would you be different if you knew the people who care about you would never leave you or stop loving you—no matter what?

## Identifying Approval-Seeking Behavior Helps Nice Guys Learn To Approve Of Themselves

As odd as it may sound, Nice Guys have to practice being themselves. One way to begin this process is to pay attention when trying to impress or get approval. Recovering Nice Guys can observe themselves spending extra time on their hair, holding the door open for someone, cleaning the kitchen, or walking with their child in the park—just to get noticed or praised.

As they become aware of how much time and energy they spend trying to garner approval, they can begin living an inside-out kind of life.

This means, rather than focusing outward for acceptance and approval, they turn inward. In doing so, they can begin asking themselves the important questions: *"What do I want," "What feels right to me," "What would make me happy?"*

Earlier in the chapter, I presented Cal as an illustration of how Nice Guys use "attachments"—things outside of themselves to get value. During a session of individual therapy, I asked Cal to make a list of things he used to get approval from others. The next week he brought in a two-page list. I encouraged him to pick one attachment from the list, and for the next month pay attention to how he used it to get value.

Cal decided to focus on his car. Cal kept his car perfectly clean, inside and out. He believed this was one of the things that impressed people and made them like him. He made a conscious decision to not wash or vacuum his car for the next month. While doing so, he would pay attention to how he felt and how people responded to him.

Since Cal lives in the Seattle area, his car soon developed a gray haze from rain and road grime. On numerous occasions, he had to fight the impulse to wash it. When he drove down the road, he was sure that people were looking at his filthy car and judging him. When he drove to work or to a friend's house, he waited for someone to shame him. When his daughter drew pictures in the dirt with her finger, it was almost more than he could stand.

At the end of the month, Cal washed and waxed his car and felt a sense of relief. Surprisingly enough, during the month not one person had commented on his dirty car, and no one had quit liking him or removed their love from him. Likewise, washing and waxing his car after a month didn't make anyone like him better or garner him any new friends.

---

## BREAKING FREE:
# ACTIVITY
## 8

Go back to the list of approval-seeking behaviors at the beginning of this chapter. Choose one of the ways you try to get external validation and do one of the following:

1. Go on a moratorium from this behavior. Set a period of time to stop doing it. Tell the people around you what you are doing. If you slip, tell a safe person about it. Use the slip as information about why, in that particular moment, you felt the need to get external approval.

2. Consciously do more of this behavior. This may not make logical sense, but it is a powerful way to explore any dysfunctional behavior. Observe how you feel when you consciously try harder to get external validation.

---

## Taking Good Care of The Self Helps Nice Guys Learn To Approve Of Themselves

Taking good care of the self is essential for changing one's belief about the self. If a Nice Guy believes he isn't worth much, his actions toward himself will reflect this belief. When a recovering Nice Guy begins to consciously do good things for himself, these actions imply that he must be worth something.

When I address this issue with Nice Guys, they frequently can't think of more than one or two good things to do for themselves. Together, we will often brainstorm and make a list of possible things to do. These good things can range from simple acts like drinking lots of water or flossing their teeth to more extensive things like taking a trip or buying the car they have always wanted. Below are a few possibilities:

- Exercise, work out, go for a walk
- Eat healthy food
- Get enough sleep
- Relax, play, goof off
- Get a massage
- Go out with buddies
- Buy a new pair of shoes
- Get shoes polished
- Get dental work done
- Get a physical
- Listen to music

As the recovering Nice Guy begins to do good things for himself, he will feel uncomfortable. He may actually feel frightened, anxious, guilty, or confused. These feelings are the result of what is called *cognitive dissonance*.

When the Nice Guy does something good for himself he is doing something that implies he is valuable. This will conflict with his deeply held belief that he is worthless. As a result, he will experience dissonance—a clashing of two competing messages. In time, one of the beliefs will win. I encourage recovering Nice Guys to keep being good to themselves, no matter how frightening. In time the core messages from childhood are replaced with new, more accurate beliefs that reflect their inherent worth.

Todd, introduced in the beginning of the chapter, spent so much time trying to get the approval of others that he rarely did anything for himself. On the encouragement of other men in his No More Mr. Nice Guy group, Todd decided to consciously begin doing things for himself. He began small by buying himself new socks and underwear.

After a few weeks, he started an exercise program and began working out regularly. Even though it made him feel guilty, he started going to a massage therapist every other week. After six months, Todd decided to spend $2,000 to join a singles activity club. He shared with the group that even though he occasionally heard a little voice that said he wasn't worth it, doing so was one of the most affirming things he had ever done. A couple of months later, he reported that he had gone on two dates with two different women, both of whom seemed to like him just as he was.

---

**BREAKING FREE:**
# ACTIVITY
## 9

Begin with the list above and add good things that you can do for yourself. Put the list up where you will see it, and choose at least one thing per day and do it for yourself.

---

## Affirming Self Helps Nice Guys
## Learn To Approve Of Themselves

Positive affirmations can help change the Nice Guy's core belief about himself. Affirmations replace old, inaccurate messages about the Nice Guy's worth with new, more realistic ones. When used alone, the affects of affirmations are usually short-lived. This is because these messages are contrary to the oldest, deepest beliefs the Nice Guy holds about himself. Affirmations are only effective when used along with other processes that help change the Nice Guy's core beliefs.

## Spending Time Alone Helps Nice Guys
## Learn To Approve Of Themselves

Spending extended time alone is an important process in recovering from the Nice Guy Syndrome. When alone, Nice Guys can discover who they are, what they like about themselves, and what rules they choose to govern their lives. I strongly recommend that Nice Guys take trips and retreats by themselves to places where no one knows them. In this context, the Nice Guy has fewer reasons to try to win people's approval, and there is less of a need to try to hide faults and mistakes. While alone, Nice Guys can reflect on themselves and their life direction. It is also a good time to practice taking responsibility for one's needs.

When alone, the recovering Nice Guy can do what he wants without having to please or compromise. He will go to bed and get up when he wants. He will decide when and what to eat. He will decide where he goes and what he does. When alone he will be less likely to caretake, seek approval, sacrifice self, or try to fix someone's problems.

Spending extended periods of time alone also helps recovering Nice Guys face their number one fear—loneliness and isolation. When the Nice Guy discovers that spending time alone doesn't kill him, he may also realize that he doesn't have to stay in bad relationships, tolerate intolerable behavior, or manipulate people to try to get his needs met.

This time alone is spent most effectively when the Nice Guy can observe his tendency to distract himself with addictive patterns, such as keeping busy, or using sex, food, or alcohol to medicate. Writing in a journal during these times can be especially effective. Some of the most insightful periods I have experienced in life have been by myself on weekend camping trips, week long retreats, and times when my wife has been out of town.

---

**BREAKING FREE:**
# ACTIVITY
## 10

Make a list of positive affirmations about yourself. Write them on note cards and place them where you will see them regularly. Change the cards often so they stay fresh. When you read affirmations, close your eyes and fully embrace the meaning of the words. Observe any tendency of your mind to reject the affirmations in favor of old, deeply held beliefs.

The following are some possible affirmations:

"I am lovable just as I am."

"I am perfectly imperfect."

"My needs are important."

"I am a strong and powerful person."

"I can handle it."

"People love and accept me just as I am."

"It is OK to be human and make mistakes."

"I am the only person I have to please."

---

## Revealing Self Helps Nice Guys Learn To Approve Of Themselves

When Nice Guys try to hide their humanity from others, they reinforce their core belief that they are bad and unlovable. Changing this core belief requires that they bring their humanity out into the open, release their toxic shame, and receive more accurate messages than the ones internalized in childhood. By necessity, this process requires a safe person or safe people.

As frightening as it may initially feel, finding these safe people is essential for learning to approve of self. The recovering Nice Guy cannot do this part alone. Safe people are essential for reversing the distorted beliefs all Nice Guys have about their worth.

This process requires building trust. I suggest that the recovering Nice Guy set a regular time to meet with his safe person or group and, a little at a time, start revealing himself. This process begins by just talking about himself. This in itself makes many Nice Guys uncomfortable. Over time, the recovering Nice Guy can begin revealing the things about himself that he is the least comfortable letting others see. Once trust has been established, he can begin to reveal things about himself that create fear and shame. I have watched many Nice Guys go from being secretive and evasive to revealing their deepest, darkest secrets in the presence of safe people.

Reid, a recovering alcoholic and a member of a No More Mr. Nice Guy group, is a good example of this process.

Reid came into a group late one evening and remained quiet and detached for the first thirty or forty minutes. Reid's pattern in the group was to either join in actively or stay withdrawn. His quiet periods were often a signal that he was emotionally distraught. When an opportune time arose I told Reid that he seemed withdrawn and I asked how he was doing.

Once the attention of the group focused on him, his appearance shifted from detachment to terror. "I almost didn't come tonight," he whispered softly as he looked down at his hands. "In fact, I was thinking about quitting the group."

A couple of the guys reflected the concern of the whole group by asking what was going on.

"I just feel so terrible," Reid continued. "I've done something so terrible, I just didn't know if I could face all of you."

My thoughts began to race as to what he could have done that might cause the group to rise up in judgment against him. One of the group members asked if he was having an affair.

"No, worse," Reid responded. "I've done something so terrible, I don't even know if I can tell you about it."

As the group offered their support and encouragement, Reid broke through his fear and shame and began to open up.

"Last week I got reprimanded by my boss and then I got into a fight with my wife. I was so depressed that I went out and bought a fifth of Vodka and got drunk. I've been on a binge ever since, and I just can't make myself stop."

Tears were running down Reid's face as the shame of his addiction to alcohol raised its ugly head once again. He had been clean and sober since joining the group six months earlier. He was active in Alcoholics Anonymous, but had experienced a number of slips and relapses in his 12 years of recovery.

A group member handed him a box of tissues and Reid wiped his eyes. He then continued telling his story and revealing his shame in between sobs.

"I'm back to all my old ways of lying and manipulating. I'm totally out of control."

I asked if he had called his sponsor or gone to a meeting since this began. He shook his head and shared that he had slipped so many times that he didn't think anyone would care or want him back.

Various members of the group shared with Reid that they didn't think he was bad nor did they judge him. They could see that he was hurting. They told him that they had great respect that he came into group and revealed what was going on, especially since he had so much shame about it.

After a few moments, Reid revealed, "That's not all. There's more." He began to sob once again. Lifting his hand to his forehead he shook his head as in disgust of himself.

"It gets worse. I went to the peep shows near my work two times this week." He turned his eyes to the floor and wept almost uncontrollably. "I had been doing so good," he choked out between sobs. "Now I've blown it all. I feel totally worthless and don't want to go on living. I've made a mess of everything."

For the rest of the hour, the group supported Reid and encouraged him to go all the way through his shame. They reassured him that he wasn't bad and that no one judged him. To the contrary, everyone respected him for revealing his shame and pain. They supported him in talking to his wife, calling his sponsor, and going to a meeting. They asked him to call one group member each day during the next week and let them know how he was doing.

When Reid left the group that night, he was obviously shaken and scared. He had also released a heavy burden and received the support of a group of people who genuinely cared about him and wanted him to be OK. No matter how deeply Reid feared that his badness would cause people to judge him and abandon him, neither of these things happened. Instead, he received the message that there was nothing he could do that would make the men in the group stop liking him or stop caring about him.

---

### BREAKING FREE:
# ACTIVITY
## 11

Plan a weekend trip to the mountains or beach. If possible, plan a vacation or retreat for a week or longer by yourself to a place where no one knows you. Visit a foreign country by yourself if at all possible. Use this time as an opportunity for self-observation and reflection. Keep a journal. Practice good selfcare. Take along this book and spend time doing the Breaking Free exercises. When you return home, observe how you are different and how long it takes for you to begin returning to familiar patterns.

---

## Shedding Old Skin

As recovering Nice Guys release their toxic shame and start seeking their own approval, they begin to realize several important truths:

- They are not bad
- They don't have to do anything to win other people's approval
- They don't have to hide their perceived flaws or mistakes
- People can love them just as they are

As recovering Nice Guys begin to apply the principles described in this chapter they can embrace the reality that they are human. Like every other human, Nice Guys make mistakes, use poor judgment, and act inappropriately. Nevertheless, their humanity doesn't make them bad or unlovable nor does it cause other people to stop loving them.

Imperfect humans can only connect with other imperfect humans. Most folks tend to be attracted to individuals who have some substance and sense of self. Chameleons usually don't draw much of a crowd or get many ovations.

By shedding their chameleon skin and learning to please themselves, recovering Nice Guys begin to experience the intimacy and connection they have always desired. By learning to approve of themselves, they begin to radiate a life energy and charisma that draws people to them. As Nice Guys stop seeking approval and stop trying to hide their perceived flaws, they open a door to start getting what they really want in love and life.

chapter # FOUR

## MAKE YOUR NEEDS
## A PRIORITY

**"I WANT YOU TO KNOW THAT
I'M REALLY UNCOMFORTABLE WITH THAT THING
WE TALKED ABOUT LAST WEEK."**

Lars, an anxiety-filled executive, began his second session of counseling with this statement. Lars had come to see me on the encouragement of his wife. He reported being generally depressed and unhappy for as long as he could remember. In recent months he had found it difficult to sleep at night and was experiencing migraine headaches on a regular basis. Even though everything in his life seemed to be "fine"—good job, nice home, family, etc.—he never seemed to be happy.

In his first counseling session, Lars revealed that he had constant fantasies of "chucking it all" and disappearing to somewhere else in the world. These thoughts made him feel guilty, so he kept them to himself.

In that session I asked Lars what he did for himself. He gave me a puzzled look. "What do you mean?" he asked.

I repeated the question.

After a pause, he answered, "Not much, I guess."

For the rest of the session, I shared with him the importance of making his needs a priority and taking responsibility for finding ways to meet them. This discussion was met with both fear and resistance from Lars. The same hesitancy was repeated as he began his second counseling session.

"Which part of our discussion last week made you uncomfortable?" I asked.

"All of it," he responded. "That part about making my needs a priority really made me uptight."

I asked him what part about taking responsibility for his needs made him anxious.

"Everything," he responded. "That seems like that would make me selfish and self-centered."

"What's wrong with that?" I asked.

Lars looked at me with amazement. "What's wrong with that," he replied, "is that being selfish would make me too much like my old man. All he ever thought about was himself, and the rest of us suffered as a result. I just couldn't do that. I couldn't be a self-centered S.O.B. like him. I've got a wife, kids, a job, a mortgage, and bills to pay. There's no room for me to start behaving like my father."

## Low Maintenance Kinds Of Guys

Lars is a fairly typical Nice Guy when it comes to his needs. Nice Guys generally focus their attention on meeting everyone else's needs while trying to be "low maintenance" kinds of guys themselves. When I talk with them about making their needs a priority, their responses are similar to that of Lars.

This ubiquitous pattern among Nice Guys is the result of childhood conditioning. When a child's needs are not met in a timely, healthy manner, the child may come to believe he is "bad" for having needs. He may also think that it is his needs that cause people to hurt him or abandon him. Typically, Nice Guys respond to these inaccurate interpretations of their life events by developing a number of survival mechanisms.

- Trying to appear needless and wantless
- Making it difficult for others to give to them
- Using "covert contracts"
- Caretaking–focusing attention on other people's needs

While creating an illusion of security in childhood, these survival mechanisms only increased the odds of their needs going unrecognized and unmet.

## Trying To Appear Needless And Wantless Prevents Nice Guys From Getting Their Needs Met

For Nice Guys, trying to become needless and wantless was a primary way of trying to cope with their childhood abandonment experiences. Since it was when they had the most needs that they felt the most abandoned, they believed it was their needs that drove people away.

These helpless little boys concluded that if they could eliminate or hide all of their needs, then no one would abandon them. They also convinced themselves that if they didn't have needs, it wouldn't hurt so bad when the needs weren't met. Not only did they learn early not to expect to get their needs met, but also that their very survival seemed to depend on appearing not to have needs.

This created an unsolvable bind: these helpless little boys could not totally repress their needs and stay alive, and they could not meet their needs on their own. The only logical solution was to try to appear to be needless and wantless while trying to get their needs met in indirect and covert ways.

As a result of these childhood survival mechanisms, Nice Guys often believe it is a virtue to have few needs or wants. Beneath this facade of needlessness and wantlessness, all Nice Guys are actually extremely needy. Consequently, when they go about trying to get their needs met, Nice Guys are frequently indirect, unclear, manipulative, and controlling.

## Making It Difficult For Others To Give To Them Prevents Nice Guys From Getting Their Needs Met

In addition to using ineffective strategies to get their needs met, *Nice Guys are terrible receivers*. Since getting their needs met contradicts their childhood paradigms, Nice Guys are extremely uncomfortable when they actually do get what they want. Though most Nice Guys have a difficult time grasping this concept, they are terrified of getting what they really want and will go to extreme measures to make sure they don't. Nice Guys carry out this unconscious agenda by connecting with needy or unavailable people, operating from an unspoken agenda, being unclear and indirect, pushing people away, and sabotaging.

A good illustration of this dynamic is the way Nice Guys commonly try to get their sexual needs met. Many of the Nice Guys I've worked with have expressed a heightened interest in sex, yet they frequently feel frustrated in their attempts to get these needs met. This is usually because their actions pretty much guarantee that they won't get what they believe they want.

Nice Guys have an uncanny knack of picking partners who, because of childhood sexual abuse or other negative experiences with sex, tend to have a difficult time being sexually expressive. When these partners do make themselves available to be sexual, it is not uncommon for Nice Guys to do something that further ensures that they don't get their needs met. The Nice Guy may respond by taking control rather than letting the sexual experience unfold. He may focus on his partner's sexual needs before she has a chance to pay attention to him. He might start a fight by making a comment about her weight or her past unavailability. All of these strategies pretty much ensure that the Nice Guy won't have to experience the fear, shame, or anxiety that might get triggered if he actually allowed someone to focus on his needs.

## Using Covert Contracts Prevents Nice Guys From Getting Their Needs Met

All Nice Guys are faced with a dilemma: How can they keep the fact that they have needs hidden, but still create situations in which they have some hope of getting their needs met?

In order to accomplish this seemingly impossible goal, Nice Guys utilize *covert contracts*. These unconscious, unspoken agreements are the primary way that Nice Guys interact with the world around them. Almost everything a Nice Guy does represents some manifestation of a covert contract.

The Nice Guy's covert contract is simply this:

*I will do this—(fill in the blank) for you, so that you will do this—(fill in the blank) for me. We will both act as if we have no awareness of this contract.*

Most of us have had the experience of leaning over and whispering in our lover's ear, "I love you." We then wait expectantly for our beloved to respond with, "I love you, too." This is an example of a covert contract in which a person gives to get. Saying "I love you" to hear "I love you, too" in return is the basic way Nice Guys go about trying to get all of their needs met. There is nothing wrong with asking your partner to tell you she loves you, but saying "I love you" first to get an "I love you, too" in return is indirect, unclear, and manipulative.

As a result of the conditioning they received in their family and society, Nice Guys believe if they are "good," then they should be loved, get their needs met, and have a problem-free life.

In reality, the primary paradigm of the Nice Guy Syndrome is nothing more than a big covert contract with life.

---

BREAKING FREE:
# ACTIVITY
## 12

Ask yourself if you believe it is OK to have needs. Do you believe people want to help you meet your needs? Do you believe this world is a place of abundance?

---

## Caretaking Prevents Nice Guys From Getting Their Needs Met

One of the most common ways Nice Guys use covert contracts to try to meet their needs is through caretaking. Nice Guys believe their caretaking is fundamentally loving, and is one of the things that makes them good people. In reality, caretaking has nothing to do with being loving or good. Caretaking is an immature and indirect attempt to try to get one's needs met.

Caretaking always consists of two parts:

*Focusing on another's problems, needs, or feelings in order to feel valuable, get one's own needs met, or to avoid dealing with one's own problems or feelings.*

Reese, a graphic designer in his late twenties, is a good example of the extremes to which Nice Guys caretake in their intimate relationships. Reese, who is gay, lamented in one of his therapy sessions, "Why can't I find a partner who gives as much back to me as I give to him?" He went on to describe how all of his boyfriends seemed to be takers and that he always did all of the giving.

Within a period of a year, Reese entered into three intense relationships. Each began wonderfully and seemed like the partnership he had been looking for. Each failed because of the same scenario:

Reese picked men who needed rescuing or fixing.

The first boyfriend lived in Canada and had recently gotten off drugs. He came to live with Reese, but he never applied for a work visa and struggled to stay clean. Reese went out of his way to be supportive of his boyfriend with the hope that he would find a job and stay off drugs. Finally, Reese sent him home to get his life straightened out. Later, he found out from a mutual friend that the reason his boyfriend had never applied for a work visa was because he was HIV positive, something he failed to tell Reese.

The next boyfriend was of a different race from Reese and had never come to grips with his homosexuality. His parents and religion kept him in constant conflict. He was never able to commit to the relationship. Nevertheless, Reese went out of his way to be supportive and giving, all with the hopes that his boyfriend would eventually get things straightened out and become available to Reese.

The third boyfriend was in the military. He was living on base, some 40 miles from Reese's apartment and had no car. Reese had to take the initiative in getting together and would often shuttle his partner around. Because Reese made more money, he always paid when they went out. Reese frequently bought his boyfriend gifts and loaned him money. When this boyfriend got transferred to a different state, Reese quit his job, sold his car, and moved along with him, only to return in three months because his partner started running around on him.

During this 12-month period while Reese was so busy caretaking the needs and problems of his boyfriends, he gave up his job and alienated most of his friends and family. Reese's caretaking allowed him to stay oblivious to his own self-destructive behaviors while investing tremendous energy in trying to fix others. As is true for most Nice Guys, no matter how much he gave to others, Reese never felt like he got as much back in return.

Identify at least one covert contract between you and a significant other. What do you give? What do you expect in return? Share this information with the other person. Ask the person how it feels to respond to an unclear agenda.

## Caring vs. Caretaking

Though Nice Guys see everything they do for others as loving, caretaking has very little to do with caring. Here are the differences:

*Caretaking*

**1.** Gives to others what the giver needs to give

**2.** Comes from a place of abundance within the giver

**3.** Always has unconscious strings attached

*Caring*

**1.** Gives to others what the receiver needs

**2.** Comes from a place of emptiness within the giver

**3.** Has no strings attached

Nice Guys caretake for a number of reasons, none of them having anything to do with love. For them, even the most innocuous and subtle act often has some string attached. Nice Guys give in the ways they would like others to give to them. They give gifts, affection, back rubs, sex, surprises. They will encourage their partner to take a day off, buy a new outfit, go to the doctor, take a trip, quit a job, go back to school—yet would not give themselves permission to do any of the same things.

# ACTIVITY
## 14

Identify two or three examples of your caretaking behavior. In order to stim-ulate awareness of your caretaking, do one of the following for a period of one week:

1. *Go on a caretaking moratorium.* Because Nice Guys have a difficult time differentiating between caring and caretaking, stop giving completely (except to young, dependent children).

Tell people what you are doing so they won't be confused. Observe your feelings and other people's reactions.

2. *Consciously try to caretake more than you already do.* As odd as this assignment may sound, it is a very effective way to create awareness of your caretaking behavior. Pay attention to how you feel and how other people react to you.

## The Victim Triangle

Rather than helping Nice Guys meet their needs, covert contracts and caretaking only lead to frustration and resentment. When this frustration and resentment builds long enough, it often spills out in some not so pretty ways. *Giving to get* creates a cycle of craziness called the *victim triangle*. The victim triangle consists of three predict-able sequences:

1. The Nice Guy gives to others hoping to get something in return.

2. When it doesn't seem that he is getting as much as he gives or he isn't getting what he expected, he feels frustrated and resentful. Remember, the Nice Guy is the one keeping score, and he isn't totally objective.

3. When this frustration and resentment builds up long enough, it spills out in the form of rage attacks, passive-aggressive behavior, pouting, tantrums, withdrawing, shaming, criticizing, blaming,

even physical abuse. Once the cycle has been completed, it usually just begins all over again.

My wife refers to these episodes as *victim pukes*. Sometimes the puking will resemble a child's temper tantrum. Sometimes the victim puke will take a more passive-aggressive form in which the Nice Guy will have an affair or act out in some hidden way. All the while the person doing the puking will feel justified because of the many ways he has been victimized. These victim pukes are one of the primary reasons Nice Guys aren't always so nice.

Shane's relationship with his girlfriend Racquel is a good example of the victim triangle and emotional puking. Shane had Racquel on a pedestal; but deep inside, he believed she could only love him if he was "good enough." In order to win her love he gave her gifts, sent her cards, left phone messages, bought her clothes, planned special surprises, and helped with her home and children.

All of this created a sense of emotional indebtedness for Racquel. She felt like she could never repay Shane for everything he did for her. The truth was she couldn't Shane was trying to buy her love—only the contract wasn't clear. In time, the only way she could cope with his pleasing and caretaking was by pushing him away.

When this happened, Shane was devastated. He couldn't understand why if he had fulfilled his end of the contract, Racquel wouldn't keep hers. He didn't think he was that hard to please. The more Shane gave to Racquel, the more resentful he became. He would accuse her of not loving him. They would have tremendous battles in which they would break up, calling each other all kinds of names. Afterward, Shane would feel frightened and remorseful and pursue Racquel and try to fix things (all the while resenting her for not pursuing him and trying to fix things). He would then start caretaking and pleasing again to win her love. The cycle repeated itself over and over again.

# ACTIVITY
## 15

It can be difficult to make a direct link between your caretaking behavior and the victim pukes which inevitably follow. Observe the ways you hurt the people you love.

- Do you make cutting remarks or hurtful "jokes"?
- Do you embarrass them in public?
- Are you frequently late?
- Do you "forget" things they've asked you to do?
- Do you criticize them?
- Do you withdraw from them or threaten to leave?
- Do you let frustration build until you blow up at them?

Ask the significant others in your life to give you feedback about your caretaking and victim pukes. This information may be hard to hear, and may trigger a shame attack, but it is important information for breaking out of the victim triangle.

## Becoming Truly Selfish

When I began writing this book, I shared the early drafts with members of my No More Mr. Nice Guy men's groups. On one occasion, a group member stated, "It seems like the whole emphasis of the book is about focusing on one's self. It seems really selfish and self-centered, like the Nice Guy should just think about himself and not worry about anyone else."

Even though I did not set out to write *No More Mr. Nice Guy* with this theme in mind, this group member's comments contained an important truth that I hadn't been fully conscious of before. *Since Nice Guys learned to sacrifice themselves in order to survive, recovery must center on learning to put themselves first and making their needs a priority.*

Most Nice Guys are astonished when I tell them that it is healthy to have needs, and that mature people make getting their needs met a priority. Sometimes I have to repeat this truth many times in order for it to sink in. For Nice Guys, having needs means being "needy," and needy represents a one-way ticket to abandonment.

I tell Nice Guys, "No one was put on this planet to meet your needs" (except their parents—and their job is done). I also remind them they weren't put on this planet to meet anyone else's needs (except those of their children).

This paradigm shift is always terrifying for recovering Nice Guys. The idea of making their needs a priority feels like the quickest route to being disliked, unloved, and all alone.

Whenever I challenge Nice Guys to focus on making their needs a priority, their responses are pretty predictable:

- "People will get angry at me."
- "People will think I'm selfish."
- "I'll be alone."
- "What if everyone lived this way?"

I then list the benefits for Nice Guys and the people around them when they begin to put themselves first:

- They increase the likelihood of getting what they need and want
- They can give judiciously–giving what people really need
- They can give without resentment and expectation
- They become less needy
- They become more attractive

Most Nice Guys will really like the last benefit on the list. Helpless, whiny, wimpy, and needy are not attractive on a man. Confidence and self-assurance are attractive. Most folks are attracted to men who have a sense of self. Putting the self first doesn't drive people away, it attracts them. Putting the self first is essential for getting what one wants in love and life.

## Taking Responsibility For Their Own Needs
## Helps Nice Guys Get Their Needs Met

In order for Nice Guys to get their needs met, they must begin to shift their core paradigms. This shift includes coming to believe:

- Having needs is part of being human.
- Mature people make meeting their own needs a priority.
- They can ask for help in meeting their needs in clear and direct ways.
- Other people really do want to help them meet their needs.
- This world is a place of abundance.

In order to get their needs met, recovering Nice Guys must do something radically different from what they have done previously. For Nice Guys, putting the self first is not just a suggestion to try on for size. It is essential not only for getting needs met, but also for reclaiming personal power, feeling fully alive, and experiencing love and intimacy.

Interestingly enough, when Nice Guys take responsibility for their own needs and make them a priority, those around them benefit too. Gone are the covert contracts, the guessing games, the anger outbursts, and passive-aggressive behavior. Gone are the manipulation, the controlling behavior, and the resentment. I learned this lesson first-hand a few years back.

A holiday weekend was approaching, and our kids were going to be out of town. I tried to plan some time with my wife Elizabeth, but she seemed ambivalent and unwilling to make a commitment to what she wanted to do. I felt frustrated and put my plans on hold. Finally, upon the urging of a friend, I decided to try putting myself first over the weekend. I made plans and invited my wife to join me if she felt inclined. I did several things I wanted to do, including spending some time with friends. As it turned out, Elizabeth decided to join me on a number of occasions. On Monday, she shared with me that she had thoroughly enjoyed the weekend and didn't want it to end.

## A Challenge

In a session of one of my No More Mr. Nice Guy men's groups, I challenged each of the group members to experiment with putting themselves first for at least a week. Though the challenge created tremendous anxiety for all of the men, each decided to accept it. The experiences of Lars, Reese, and Shane are presented below.

### Lars

Lars, introduced at the beginning of the chapter, went home after the group and told his wife that he was going to make his needs a priority for the following week. She was initially resistant to his proclamation, which added to his anxiety. To boost his courage, Lars called a couple of men in the group. Their encouragement gave him the support he needed to follow through with his commitment.

Lars decided to keep it simple. His plan for the week involved making time every day to go the gym and work out. Before his children were born, Lars had been physically active. The demands of job, home, and children had put an end to that. Lars decided to alternate his workouts before and after work. When he shared his plan with his wife, she applied a little guilt. "That's not fair that you get to work out and I don't," she proclaimed. Lars was tempted to back down. He had an impulse to try to find a solution so his wife could work out, too. Instead, he reflected on her concern and told her he was going to work out anyway.

During his first couple of trips to the gym, Lars was overwhelmed with guilt and anxiety. Nevertheless, he persevered. After the third day, his wife actually asked him how his workout went. As the week continued, Lars began to feel more energized and optimistic about life. He started sleeping better. At the gym, he enjoyed being around other people who were also taking good care of themselves. Surprisingly, after his first week, his wife told him that he had inspired her to start taking better care of herself. She told him that she was going to start dropping the kids off at the daycare center at the gym and begin an aerobics class for herself.

### Reese

Reese had joined the No More Mr. Nice Guy group after his breakup with his last boyfriend. At first he had been uncomfortable being the only gay man in the group, but the other men accepted him, and he had begun to work on developing nonsexual relationships with men.

Reese's habit on weekends was to go to out with his latest boyfriend to gay bars on Friday, Saturday, and Sunday nights. By Monday morning, he was exhausted. He would spend the rest of the week playing catch up. Reese was afraid that if he didn't go out whenever his boyfriend wanted, his boyfriend would leave him.

Reese decided that for one weekend, he would put himself first and do what felt right to him. He told his boyfriend in advance. Reese decided that he would go out just one night, not drink, and be in by midnight. On Saturday, he made some plans to go to a movie with a couple of guys in the group. On Sunday he stayed at home to relax and get caught up on some house cleaning and laundry. His goal was to be in bed by 10:00 p.m. on Sunday evening.

When Monday came, Reese felt rested and clear headed at work. His boyfriend hadn't dropped him, and the rest of the week felt productive and enjoyable.

### Shane

Shane, also introduced earlier in the chapter, liked to do things for his girlfriend. Shane regularly gave her gifts, planned surprises, and did whatever he could to help her out.

Shane's plan for putting himself first involved paying attention to when he had an impulse to do something for his girlfriend. Whenever he felt this impulse, he would instead do something for himself. When he thought about washing her car, he washed his own instead. When he felt the urge to buy her a gift, he bought himself something instead. When he thought about calling her just to see if she was OK, he called a group member instead. All of this created tremendous anxiety for Shane.

Much to his surprise, at the end of the week Racquel reported she felt a lot less smothered by Shane and actually looked forward to spending time with him. She even called late one evening after the kids were in bed and invited him over to make love.

A couple of weeks later, Shane and Racquel talked about the change in a couples counseling session. They decided to continue the process. For a period of six months they agreed that Shane would not give any gifts or plan any surprises for Racquel. During the following six months he refrained from giving her birthday, Christmas, and Valentine's cards or gifts. During this time he focused on taking better care of himself and getting his needs met.

In time Shane came to see that not only did Racquel not stop loving him, she actually became more giving to Shane. One year later, they both reported that Shane could give a gift without using it as a way to get approval or affirmation. During this time, Shane had also learned that making his needs a priority made him less dependent, needy, and fearful. Both Shane and Racquel reported enjoying all the changes they had experienced since Shane made the decision to start putting himself first.

## Making The Decision

Nice Guys have believed a myth that promises them that if they give up themselves and put others first, they will be loved and get their needs met. There is only one way to change this illogical, nonproductive Nice Guy paradigm—*to put themselves first.*

Making the decision to put one's self first is the hardest part. Actually doing it is relatively easy. When the Nice Guy puts himself first there is only one voice to consider—his own. Decisions are now made by one individual, rather than by a committee. He no longer has to mind read, predict, or try to please multiple voices with conflicting agendas. When putting himself first, all the information he needs to make a decision is within him: "Is this what I want? Yes. Then that's what I'll do."

Breaking free from the Nice Guy Syndrome involves taking responsibility for one's own needs. Others may cooperate with the Nice Guy, but they are not in charge of meeting his needs. By making their needs a priority and putting themselves first, recovering Nice Guys can come to see the world as a place of abundance. They can truly come to believe that their needs are important, and there are people out there who are happy and willing to help them meet them.

---

**BREAKING FREE:**
# ACTIVITY
## 16

Make a decision to put yourself first for a weekend or even a whole week. Tell the people around you what you are doing. Ask a friend to support you and encourage you in this process. Pay attention to your initial anxiety. Pay attention to your tendency to revert to old patterns. At the end of the time period, ask the people around you what it was like for them when you put yourself first.

Remember, you don't have to do it perfectly. Just do it.

---

# FIVE

## RECLAIM YOUR PERSONAL POWER

One Saturday morning a few years back, my wife Elizabeth and I were engaged in a heated discussion over something I had done. Like many of our arguments, Elizabeth felt helpless to get me to see my denial. At the same time, I felt unjustly persecuted. Finally, when the argument reached an emotional crescendo, Elizabeth shouted in frustration,

"You're nothing but a wimp!"

Elizabeth left the room and I retreated to the bathroom to dry my eyes.

After a few minutes of reflection, Elizabeth knocked on the bathroom door. I assumed she was coming back to take another stab at her wounded prey. Instead, she apologized.

"I'm sorry for calling you a wimp. That wasn't fair."

"Actually," I responded, wiping a tear away, "It was the most accurate thing you said all morning."

Nice Guys are wimps. This may not sound like a nice thing to say, but it's true. Nice Guys tend to be wimpy victims because their life paradigm and childhood survival mechanisms require them to sacrifice their personal power.

As stated in previous chapters, a common denominator for Nice Guys is that they did not get their needs met in a timely, healthy fashion in childhood. These little boys were helpless to prevent people from abandoning them, neglecting them, abusing them, using them, or smothering them. They were victims to the people who failed to love them, pay attention to them, meet their needs, and protect them.

As a result of these childhood experiences, feeling like a victim feels familiar for most Nice Guys. These men tend to see others as causing the problems they are experiencing in life. As a consequence, they often feel frustrated, helpless, resentful, and rageful. You can see it in their body language. You can hear it in their voices:

"It's not fair."

"How come she gets to make the rules?"

"I always give more than I get."

"If she would just...."

## A Paradigm Of Powerlessness

In an attempt to cope with their childhood abandonment experiences, all Nice Guys developed the same paradigm: "If I am good, then I will be loved, get my needs met, and have a problem-free life." Unfortunately, this paradigm not only produces the opposite of what is desired, it guarantees nothing but feelings of perpetual powerlessness.

Even though Nice Guys are obsessed with trying to create a smooth, problem-free life, two major factors prevent them from attaining this goal. The first is that they are attempting the impossible. Life is not smooth. Human existence is by nature chaotic. Life is filled with experiences that are unpredictable and beyond anyone's control. Therefore, trying to create a predictable life in which everything always goes as planned is an exercise in futility.

In spite of the fact that we live in a chaotic, unpredictable world, Nice Guys are not only convinced that life can be smooth, they believe it should be. This belief is the direct result of their childhood abandonment experiences. The unpredictability of not having their needs met in a timely, judicious fashion was not only frightening, it was potentially life-threatening.

*In an attempt to cope with the uncertainty of their chaotic childhoods, Nice Guys developed a belief system that if they could just do everything right, then everything would go right in their lives.* Sometimes these men also developed belief systems that their childhood was ideal and problem-free (the opposite of reality) in order to cope with their abandonment experiences. These were all distorted beliefs, but these illusions helped these helpless little boys deal with the turmoil that was out of their control.

A second reason Nice Guys never accomplish their goal of having a smooth life is that they do the opposite of what works. By approaching adult situations with survival mechanisms that were formed when they were naive and powerless, they are assured of having very little success in creating anything that resembles stability in their lives.

The dependence on these ineffective survival mechanisms keeps Nice Guys trapped in the memory of their fearful childhood experiences and perpetuates a vicious cycle. The more frightened they are, the more they use their childhood survival mechanisms. The more they use these ineffective mechanisms, the less successful they are at negotiating the complexities, challenges, and ambiguities of life. The less successful they are, the more fearful they become . . . you get the picture.

# Overcoming The Wimp Factor—
# Reclaiming Personal Power

I define *personal power* as a state of mind in which a person is confident he can handle whatever may come. This kind of power not only successfully deals with problems, challenges and adversity, it actually welcomes them, meets them head on, and is thankful for them. Personal power isn't the absence of fear. Even the most powerful people have fear. Personal power is the result of feeling fear, but not giving in to the fear.

There is a solution to the helplessness and vulnerability Nice Guys feel. Recovery from the Nice Guy Syndrome allows Nice Guys to embrace the personal power that is their birthright. Reclaiming personal power includes:

- Surrendering
- Dwelling in reality
- Expressing feelings
- Facing fears
- Developing integrity
- Setting boundaries

---

**BREAKING FREE:**
# ACTIVITY
## 17

Look over the following list of ways Nice Guys try to create a smooth, problem-free life. Write down an example of how you used each coping mechanism in childhood. Then, next to each, give an example of how you use this strategy to try to control your world in adulthood. Note how each of these behaviors keep you feeling like a powerless victim. Share this information with a safe person.

- Doing it right
- Playing it safe

- Anticipating and fixing
- Trying not to rock the boat
- Being charming and helpful
- Never being a moment's problem
- Using covert contracts
- Controlling and manipulating
- Caretaking and pleasing
- Withholding information
- Repressing feelings
- Making sure other people don't have feelings
- Avoiding problems and difficult situations

---

## Surrendering Helps Nice Guys Reclaim Their Personal Power

Ironically, the most important aspect of reclaiming personal power and getting what one wants in love and life is *surrender*. Surrender doesn't mean giving up. It means letting go of what one can't change and changing what one can.

Letting go doesn't mean not caring or not trying. Letting go means letting be. It is like opening up a tightly clenched fist and releasing the tension stored inside. At first the fingers will want to return to their former clenched position. The hand almost has to be retrained to open up and relax. So it is with learning how to surrender and let go.

Surrender allows recovering Nice Guys to let go and respond to life's complex beauty, rather than trying to control it. Surrender allows these men to see life as a laboratory for learning, growth, and creativity. *Surrender allows recovering Nice Guys to see each life experience as a "gift" from the universe to stimulate growth, healing, and learning.* Instead of asking, "Why is this happening to me?" the recovering Nice Guy can respond to life's challenges by pondering, "What do I need to learn from this situation?"

Gil exemplifies the process of letting go. Gil had reached a crisis point in his relationship with his girlfriend Barb. Gil had originally begun couples counseling with Barb to "fix" her problem. He claimed that she was depressed, angry all the time, and had no interest in sex. He reported that he constantly walked on eggshells, trying to make sure he never did anything to upset her.

Gil and Barb were both in their early fifties and had been living together for eight years. They had discussed marriage, but both felt apprehension due to the unsettled nature of their relationship. After a couple months of couples counseling, Gil began to entertain the idea that all the problems in the relationship might not be about Barb. He began looking at his own caretaking and controlling behavior. He also became aware that he had few outside interests and no male friends. After a couple more months, he joined a No More Mr. Nice Guy men's group.

Even as Gil began to look at his own problems and ineffective life patterns, he kept seeking the "key" for making Barb better. It was a slow process, but Gil began to see that he could not do anything to change Barb, and that he was going to have to focus on himself. As he began to let go and detach from Barb he felt tremendous anxiety. He had a deep fear that he was going to "get in trouble." He also believed that Barb couldn't handle her problems without his help.

With the support of the group, Gil surrendered. He came to realize that he would be OK regardless of whether he and Barb made it as a couple. Much to his surprise, their relationship began to improve. As he let go of trying to solve her problems and detached from her moods, Gil found that he had fewer frustrations and resentments. He even began to see Barb as a "gift" to help him work through his issues with his angry father.

A year later he announced to his men's group that he and Barb had set a date to get married. He reported that they were getting along better than he would have ever imagined. He shared that the turning point seemed to be when he made the decision that he didn't care whether they made it together or not. That decision represented a conscious letting go of trying to control something that was clearly not in his control. Ironically, he shared that the process of letting go allowed him to receive what he really wanted.

---

**BREAKING FREE:**
# ACTIVITY
## 18

Think about one "gift" from the universe that you initially resisted but can now see as a positive stimulus for growth or discovery.

Are there any similar gifts in your life right now to which you need to surrender?

Share this information with a safe person.

---

## Dwelling In Reality Helps Nice Guys Reclaim Their Personal Power

Nice Guys try to control their world by creating belief systems about people and situations that are not based in reality. They then act as if these beliefs are accurate. This is why their behavior often seems illogical to outside observers.

Les, an unassuming man in his late thirties, had a brief affair with a co-worker. During his initial therapy session, I asked Les why he thought he had an affair. "I don't know," he replied. "I guess I just wanted some attention."

I continued by asking him how he expressed his anger toward his wife. With a puzzled look, he responded, "I never get angry at Sarah."

"You mean you two have been married for 10 years and she's never done anything to piss you off?" I asked in mock surprise.

To listen to Les talk about his wife, it was evident he had her on a pedestal. It was equally clear that he was not dwelling in reality when it came to his marriage. When I asked specific questions about his wife, Les revealed how Sarah had gained 60 pounds since they married, refused to cook, was depressed, no longer wanted to have sex with him, treated him with contempt, and would rage at him without provocation. In spite of all these things, Les maintained that his wife was the woman of his dreams, and that he loved her dearly.

Throughout the next few months of therapy, I consistently held up a mirror of reality to Les in regard to his wife and his relationship with her. This was a slow and difficult process. Les needed to see Sarah in a certain way because of his fear of being alone. To dwell in reality might mean he would have to do something frightening or difficult.

As Les began to face his fears of abandonment he also began to see his wife more accurately. This change allowed him to start asking for what he wanted, set boundaries, and express his feelings of resentment and anger. It soon became apparent that Sarah had no desire to look at her role in the relationship or make any kind of changes. Though it was painful and frightening, accepting things as they really were allowed Les to make the decision to move out and file for divorce.

Dwelling in reality allowed Les to look at why he had created the kind of system he had with Sarah. It put him in a position to make difficult but realistic decisions. It allowed him to access the inner power he needed to make significant changes in his life. It also opened the door for him to find someone who was available to help him create the kind of relationship he wanted.

---

BREAKING FREE:
## ACTIVITY
### 19

Pick one area in your life in which you routinely feel frustrated or out of control. Step back from the situation. Is the difficulty you are having with the situation the result of you trying to project the reality you want to believe onto it? If you had to accept the reality of this situation, how might you change your response to it?

---

## Expressing Feelings Helps Nice Guys Reclaim Their Personal Power

Nice Guys are terrified of two kinds of feelings—their own and everyone else's. Any kind of intensity causes Nice Guys to feel out of control. As children, feeling things intensely invited either negative attention or no attention at all. Therefore, it came to feel safer to clamp a lid down tightly on any emotion that might attract too much negative attention or might cause them to feel abandoned.

I remember early in our marriage when Elizabeth would express her frustration over my inability to share what I was feeling. Like most Nice Guys, I had come to see feelings as a dangerous thing. After more than 30 years of conditioning, I had no clue what Elizabeth wanted from me.

Even as I began to become aware of my feelings, I often kept them to myself. It is almost comical how infrequently it crosses a Nice Guy's mind to tell his partner what he is feeling. On one occasion, Elizabeth confronted me when I shared a feeling with her that I had been harboring for some time. "Why didn't you tell me about that when you first felt it?" she questioned.

"I'm doing better," I replied in typical Nice Guy fashion. "It only took me two weeks to get around to telling you."

I frequently hear Nice Guys rationalize the withholding of their feelings by claiming they don't want to hurt anyone. The truth is they are covering their own butts. What they are really saying is that they don't want to do anything that might re-create their childhood experiences. They're really not trying to protect anyone from harm, they're just trying to keep their world smooth and under control.

I frequently tell Nice Guys, "Your feelings are just feelings, they won't kill you." Regardless of whether a Nice Guy is feeling anxious, helpless, shameful, lonely, rageful, or sad, his feelings aren't life threatening.

The goal of teaching Nice Guys to embrace their feelings is not to make them soft and "touchy feely." Men who are in touch with their feelings are powerful, assertive, and energized. Contrary to what many Nice Guys believe, they don't have to become more like women in order to have their feelings. This is why I support men in learning about their feelings from other men.

While there is no formula, or "right" way to get reconnected with repressed feelings, support groups can teach, model, and support this slow, but important process. In a sense, a therapy group can become like a family. In this environment, recovering Nice Guys can ask for the kind of help in dealing with feelings that was never available to them as children. Since feelings are often messy, a group environment can represent a supportive place to momentarily feel out of control. Here, recovering Nice Guys find out they won't fall overboard and drown if they rock the boat. They also learn that they won't shrivel up and die if someone else around them has a feeling.

Feelings are an integral part of human existence. By learning the language of feelings, recovering Nice Guys can begin to let go of a lifetime of unnecessary baggage. As they do, they experience a new-found energy, optimism, intimacy, and zest for life.

This reality hit home with me a few years ago in a very unexpected way. Elizabeth came to me one day and revealed that she had backed into a parked car. She felt like a bad little child and waited for me to scold her. Even before I had a chance to respond, she began to put up a wall and withdraw as a way of protecting herself.

I got angry—not about the car, but about the manner in which she was pushing me away. I expressed my feelings clearly and directly. Without shaming or attacking, I said "Stop." With an intensity of emotion that surprised both of us, I let her know that I wasn't pushing her away, and I wasn't going to accept her pushing me away. I told her that I did have feelings about the car, but I had even stronger feelings about how she was acting. I said, "Just let me have my feelings about the car, and then we'll work it out."

Later, Elizabeth revealed to me (and several of her friends) how much safer she felt when I had my feelings. She was able to hear that I was upset about the car but that I didn't think she was bad, and I wasn't going to abandon her. The fact that I had such intensity about not letting her push me away actually made her feel secure and loved. As a result, she felt safe to stay connected to me and hear my feelings about the car. The whole incident brought us closer, and has since provided a reference point for the healing power of expressing emotions in powerful and direct ways.

---

**BREAKING FREE:**
# ACTIVITY
## 20

Some guidelines about expressing feelings:

- Don't focus on the other person, "You are making me mad."
  Instead, take responsibility for what you are feeling, "I am feeling angry."
- Don't use feeling words to describe what you are thinking, as in
  "I feel like Joe was trying to take advantage of me."
- Instead, pay attention to what you are experiencing in your body,
  "I'm feeling helpless and frightened."
- In general, try to begin feeling statements with "I," rather than "you."
  Try to avoid the crutch of saying "I feel like." As in, "I feel like you are being mean to me."

---

## Facing Fears Helps Nice Guys Reclaim Their Personal Power

Fear is a normal part of human experience. Everyone experiences fear, even those people who seem to be fearless. Healthy fear is a warning sign that danger may be approaching. This is different from the fear Nice Guys experience on a daily basis.

For Nice Guys, fear is recorded at the cellular level. It is a memory of every seemingly life-threatening experience they ever had. It was born of a time of absolute dependency and helplessness. It originated in not having their needs met in a timely, judicious manner. It was fostered by fearful systems that discouraged risk and rewarded conservatism. It was heightened by the reality that life is messy and chaotic and any kind of change promises a journey into the unknown. I call this kind of fear *Memory Fear*.

Because of the memory fear created in childhood, Nice Guys still approach the world as if it is dangerous and overpowering. To cope with these realities, Nice Guys typically hunker down and play it safe.

As a consequence of playing it safe, Nice Guys experience a lot of needless suffering.

- Suffering because they avoid new situations
- Suffering because they stay with the familiar
- Suffering because they procrastinate, avoid, and fail to finish what they start
- Suffering because they make a bad situation worse by doing more of what has never worked in the past
- Suffering because they expend so much energy trying to control the uncontrollable

Nolan is a good example of the paralyzing effect of memory fear. Nolan came to see me on the recommendation of a friend. He had been separated from his wife for a year but was having a difficult time making a final decision about getting divorced.

Nolan frequently told me he was "confused." This confusion was mixed with a strong dose of guilt. Nolan constantly weighed all the issues. What if he left his wife and later realized that it was a mistake? What if he messed up his kids' lives? What if his children never wanted to talk to him again? What if his friends thought he was bad? What if God sent him to hell? As long as Nolan stayed "confused" about what he should do, he remained paralyzed.

When I told Nolan that I didn't think he was confused but that he was afraid, he was initially defensive. He didn't like seeing himself as being fearful. As we explored the memory fear from his childhood, he came to realize that any mistakes he made as a child seemed to have everlasting consequences. He believed the same would be true in his present situation.

Behind Nolan's fear of making a decision was the childhood fear that he wouldn't be able to handle whatever happened. Together we brainstormed all the possible consequences of divorcing his wife. Behind each potential consequence was the unconscious belief that he wouldn't be able to handle it.

I sent Nolan home with his list of fears along with a more accurate statement about each: *No matter what happened, he would handle it*. The following week, Nolan proudly announced that he had contacted an attorney. Even though he felt tremendous fear and anxiety, he found courage in repeating his new found mantra: "*I can handle it.*"

Facing present day fears is the only way to overcome memory fear. Every time the Nice Guy confronts a fear, he unconsciously creates a belief that he can handle whatever it is he is afraid of. This challenges his memory fear. Challenging this memory fear makes the things outside of him seem less threatening. As these things seem less frightening, he feels more confident in confronting them. The more this confidence grows, the less threatening life seems.

## Developing Integrity Helps Nice Guys Reclaim Their Personal Power

Most Nice Guys pride themselves on being honest and trustworthy. In reality, Nice Guys are fundamentally dishonest. They have the ability to tell a lie or withhold the truth and still believe the illusion that they are basically honest people. Since dishonesty is a fear-based behavior, telling lies and withholding the truth robs Nice Guys of their personal power.

I define lying as anything less than the truth. This may seem evident to most people, but it is important to define "lying" and "telling the truth" because Nice Guys are adept at creating definitions that justify their behavior. It is not unusual to hear them make statements like "I'm pretty honest" or "I'm honest most of the time" without the slightest awareness of their contradiction of terms. In an almost childlike manner, Nice Guys will often offer the following defense: "I didn't lie, I just didn't tell everything."

Joel was the owner of a successful construction company. On occasion, he would leave work a little early and catch an afternoon movie before heading home. Because he feared his wife's disapproval, he would refrain from telling her how he spent those afternoons. He would always have some cover story ready in case she tried to call him while he was out. The irony of the situation is that there was absolutely no reason for Joel to lie to his wife. In spite of all the effort Joel put into hiding the truth of his whereabouts, it never crossed his mind that he was lying to himself and to his wife. The bottom line was that Joel's lying perpetuated a fear-based relationship with his wife and robbed him of his personal power.

When Nice Guys are learning to tell the truth, I encourage them to pay attention to the things they least want others to know, and what they least want to reveal. These are the things they are most likely to hold back—and the things they most need to tell. Sometimes they have to practice telling a certain truth several times until all of these pieces of information get told.

Sometimes after telling the truth, Nice Guys will report that it was a "mistake" because someone reacted with anger. Telling the truth is not a magic formula for having a smooth life. But living a life of integrity is actually easier than living one built around deceit and distortion.

Developing integrity is an essential part of recovery from the Nice Guy Syndrome.

My definition of integrity is about deciding what feels right and doing it.

The alternative is using the "committee approach." This method of decision-making and acting is based on trying to guess what everyone else would think is right. Following this committee approach is the quickest path to confusion, fear, powerlessness, and dishonesty.

When applying the definition above, there are two ways to be *out of* integrity, but only one way to be *in* it. When a Nice Guy never even bothers to ask himself, "What do I think is right?" or uses the committee method, he will always be out of integrity. If he asks himself what he believes is right but doesn't do it, he is also out of integrity. Only by asking himself what he believes is right, and then doing it, does he become a man of integrity.

---

**BREAKING FREE:**
# ACTIVITY
## 21

List one fear that has been controlling your life. Once you decide to confront the fear, begin repeating to yourself, "I can handle it. No matter what happens, I will handle it." Keep repeating this mantra until you take action and stop feeling fear.

---

**BREAKING FREE:**
# ACTIVITY
## 22

Choose one area in which you have been out of integrity. Identify your fear that keeps you from telling the truth or doing the right thing. Reveal this situation to a safe person. Then go and tell the truth, or do what you have to do to make the situation right. Tell yourself you can handle it. Since telling the truth may create a crisis for you or others, have faith that everyone involved will survive this crisis.

## Setting Boundaries Helps Nice Guys Reclaim Their Personal Power

Boundaries are essential for survival. Learning to set boundaries allows Nice Guys to stop feeling like helpless victims and reclaim their personal power. Boundary setting is one of the most fundamental skills I teach to recovering Nice Guys.

I demonstrate the concept of boundaries by laying a shoestring on the ground. I tell the Nice Guy that I am going to cross his boundary and push him backwards. I instruct him to stop me when he begins to feel uncomfortable. It is not unusual for a Nice Guy to stand well back from the line, allowing me to violate his space several steps before he even begins to respond. Once I start pushing, it's not uncommon for a Nice Guy to let me push him back several steps before he does anything to stop me. Sometimes a Nice Guy will let me push him all the way to the wall.

I use this exercise as a graphic demonstration of the need for boundaries in all areas of life. Nice Guys are usually more comfortable backpedaling, giving in, and keeping the peace. They believe if they take one more step backward, the other person will quit pushing and then everything will be smooth.

It is not unusual for recovering Nice Guys to go a little overboard when they first learn about boundary setting. They have a tendency to swing from one extreme to another. They become Kamikaze boundary setters. They try to set boundaries with a sledge hammer or machete. They usually learn in time that they only have to use as much resistance as necessary to get the job done.

In time, they also learn that boundary setting isn't about getting other people to be different. It's about getting themselves to be different. If someone is crossing their boundary, it isn't the other person's problem; it is theirs.

Because of memory fear, Nice Guys often unconsciously reinforce the very behaviors they find intolerable. *Due to their childhood conditioning, they teach the people around them that they will accept having their boundaries violated.* As recovering Nice Guys begin to take responsibility for how they let people treat them, their own behavior begins to change. As they stop reinforcing things they aren't willing to tolerate, the people around them are given the opportunity to behave differently. This gives relationships a chance to survive and grow.

Jake, an enlisted man in his mid twenties, is a good example of how tolerating intolerable behavior can kill a relationship, and how setting boundaries can give a relationship a chance to survive.

Just prior to his marriage to his wife Kisha, Kisha had an affair with an old boyfriend. Because Jake didn't want to lose her, he forgave her and promised to never bring up her infidelity. This established a pattern of Kisha pretty much doing whatever she wanted while Jake withheld his feelings and walked on eggshells. He would always measure his words in order to avoid saying anything "wrong" that might upset her.

On one occasion, while they were out drinking with some friends, Kisha got drunk. Whenever she had too much to drink she would become belligerent and promiscuous. On this occasion, she made several demeaning remarks to Jake and spent most of the evening slow dancing with other men in the bar.

After holding his tongue as long as he could, Jake finally told Kisha that she was drunk, and that it was time to go home. She swore at him and kept on doing what she was doing. Jake retaliated by calling her a "bitch" and drove home.

One of her friends brought Kisha home the next morning. For

the rest of the day she gave Jake the silent treatment. He tried to hold out, but after a few hours of misery, he apologized for calling her a bitch.

Later that week, he somewhat reluctantly talked about the episode in his No More Mr. Nice Guy group. The group members lovingly confronted him. They pointed out how his willingness to tolerate his wife's intolerable behavior gave her license to act in any way she pleased. They told Jake that the problem was not Kisha, it was him. Until Jake changed, his wife would have no incentive to change. By not setting boundaries he was robbing his marriage of the opportunity to become what it could be.

---

**BREAKING FREE:**
# ACTIVITY
## 23

Before you can start setting boundaries, you have to become aware of how much you back up from your line to avoid conflict or to keep the peace. For the next week, observe yourself. Do you say "yes" when you would rather say "no"? Do you agree to do something to avoid conflict? Do you avoid doing something because someone might get upset at you? Do you tolerate an intolerable situation, hoping that it will just go away? Write these observations down and share them with a safe person.

---

The next day, Jake confronted his wife. He acknowledged his role in their situation. He told her that he was no longer going to tolerate intolerable behavior. He told her his boundaries. He would no longer tolerate Kisha dancing or flirting with other men. He would not tolerate her demeaning him in front of their friends. He told her that if she wanted to stay married to him, she had to go to treatment for her drinking problem.

Kisha responded by telling Jake that no one was going to tell her what to do. She packed a bag and moved out that night to a friend's house. Even though Jake was miserable the next few days, he resisted the temptation to call her and beg her to come back. Instead, he called some guys in the group.

Three nights later, Kisha called and said she wanted to talk. She came over and told Jake that even though she initially wanted to tell him to go to hell, she knew he was right. For the first time in their marriage, she said she felt respect for him. She said she wanted to save their marriage and was willing to do whatever it took to make it work. The following week Kisha entered treatment.

## Take A Walk On The Wild Side

There is no "key" to a smooth life. Being "good" or doing it "right" doesn't insulate Nice Guys from the chaotic, ever-changing realities of life. All the Nice Guy paradigm does is create wimpy men who allow bullies to kick sand in their face or shame them for loading the dishwasher "wrong."

As recovering Nice Guys begin to surrender, dwell in reality, express their feelings, face their fears, develop integrity, and set boundaries, they access a power that allows them to welcome and embrace the challenges and "gifts" of life. Life isn't a merry-go-round, it's a roller coaster. As they reclaim personal power, recovering Nice Guys can experience the world in all of its serendipitous beauty. Life won't always be smooth, it may not always be pretty, but it will be an adventure—one not to be missed.

# chapter SIX

# RECLAIM YOUR MASCULINITY

**CONTRARY TO THE PREVAILING SENTIMENTS OF THE
LAST FEW DECADES, IT IS OK TO BE A GUY.**

M en born after World War II had the misfortune of growing up
during the only era of recent Western history in which it was
not always a good thing to be male. This was primarily the
result of two significant family and social changes in the post war era:
boys were disconnected from their fathers and other healthy male
role models, and boys were forced to seek approval from women and
accept a female definition of what it meant to be male.

As a result of these two dynamics, many boys and men came to
believe that they had to hide or eliminate any negative male traits
(like those of their fathers or other "bad" men) and become what they
believed women wanted them to be. For many men, this life strategy
seemed essential if they wanted to be loved, get their needs met, and
have a smooth life.

Due to the continuing social change of the last half of the twentieth century, this belief system is no longer limited to just men of

the Baby Boom generation. I frequently observe men in their thirties, twenties, and teens, with strong Nice Guy traits. It seems that each successive generation of men are becoming more and more passive.

This social conditioning affects Nice Guys in many ways:

- Nice Guys tend to be disconnected from other men.
- Nice Guys tend to be disconnected from their own masculinity.
- Nice Guys tend to be monogamous to their mothers.
- Nice Guys tend to be dependent on the approval of women.

## Nice Guys Tend To Be Disconnected From Other Men

I frequently hear Nice Guys make comments such as:

- "I'm just not comfortable with other men. I don't know what to talk about."
- "Most men are jerks."
- "I used to have male friends, but my wife made it such a hassle to do things with them that I just gave up."
- "I tend to be a loner."

Many Nice Guys have difficulty connecting with men because of the limited positive male contact they experienced in childhood. Because these men did not have a positive bond with their father, they never learned the basic skills necessary to build meaningful relationships with men.

Another common trait among Nice Guys is the belief that they are different from other men. This distorted thinking usually began in childhood, when they tried to be different from their "bad" or unavailable father. In adulthood, Nice Guys often create a similar dynamic with men in general. Nice Guys may convince themselves they are different from (better than) other men because they believe:

- They aren't controlling
- They aren't angry and rageful
- They aren't violent
- They are attentive to a woman's needs
- They are good lovers
- They are good fathers

As long as Nice Guys are disconnected from men or believe they are different from other men, they cut themselves off from the many positive benefits of male companionship and the power of a masculine community.

---

Look over the list above. Note the ways you have consciously or unconsciously tried to be different from your father and/or other men. How does the belief that you are different keep you disconnected from other men?

---

## Nice Guys Tend To Be
## Disconnected From Their Masculinity

I define masculinity as *that part of a man that equips him to survive as an individual, clan, and species.* Without this masculine energy we would have all become extinct eons ago. Masculinity empowers a man to create and produce. It also empowers him to provide for and protect those who are important to him. These aspects of masculinity include strength, discipline, courage, passion, persistence, and integrity.

Masculine energy also represents the potential for aggressiveness, destructiveness, and brutality. These characteristics frighten Nice Guys—and most women—therefore Nice Guys work especially hard to repress these traits.

Most Nice Guys believe that by repressing the darker side of their masculine energy they will win the approval of women. This seems logical considering the anti-male climate that has permeated our culture since the 1960s. Ironically, these same men frequently complain that women seemed to be attracted to "jerks" rather than Nice Guys like them. Many women have shared with me that due to the absence of any discernible life energy in Nice Guys, there is little to be attracted to. They also reveal that their tendency to be attracted to "jerks" is because these men have more of a masculine edge to them.

As Nice Guys try to avoid the dark side of their masculinity, they also repress many other aspects of this male energy force. As a result, they often lose their sexual assertiveness, competitiveness, creativity, ego, thirst for experience, boisterousness, exhibitionism, and power. Go watch little boys on the playground and you will see these qualities. I am convinced that these are good things worth keeping.

One of the most visible consequences of the repression of masculine energy in Nice Guys is their lack of leadership in their families. Out of fear of upsetting their partner or appearing too much like their controlling, authoritarian, or abusive fathers, Nice Guys frequently fail to be the leader their family needs. Consequently, the job of leading the family often falls on their wives. Most of the women I talk to don't want this job, but end up taking it by default.

## Nice Guys Tend To Be Monogamous To Their Mothers

Becoming and remaining monogamous to their mothers is a common pattern for Nice Guys. This unconscious bond is the result of a normal childhood developmental phenomenon gone amuck. Let me explain.

All little boys naturally fall in love with their mother and desire to have her all to themselves. Healthy mothers and fathers help their sons successfully move through this normal developmental stage. As they do, the young boy individuates from his mother, bonds with men, and becomes available for an intimate relationship with another woman in adulthood.

Each parent plays a significant role in facilitating this healthy transition. First, the mother must know how to give enough to meet the child's needs without creating dependency. She must also know how to get her own needs met so she is not tempted to use her son to fill the void. Second, the father must be present and have a healthy bond with his son. This connection helps the little boy move from the cozy lap of his mother to the challenging world of men.

As stated above, most Nice Guys do not report having had a close relationship with their father in childhood. As a result, many Nice Guys were forced into an unhealthy bond with their mother. This bond might have formed if they had to please an angry, critical, or controlling mother. More often than not, the bond was the result of being forced to take care of a needy, dependent, or smothering mother. Without a supportive father, these boys had to negotiate an impossible situation on their own.

Both childhood situations—trying to please an angry or controlling mother, or becoming mother's little partner—created a dynamic in which Nice Guys unconsciously became monogamous to their mothers and did not individuate in a healthy way.

When a Nice Guy has been conditioned to be monogamous to his mother in childhood, his adult partner will know at some level that he is not really available. The partner may not consciously connect this to his bond with his mother, but she knows something is missing.

Anita, a woman in her late fifties, was married to a man who was monogamous to his mother. I met Anita when she called and made an appointment for individual counseling. She believed her husband was having an affair, and she wanted some advice. As we began our session she sat down on the couch and smiled nervously.

"I feel so foolish coming here, but I just don't know who to talk to. I feel crazy, because I think my husband is having an affair with his secretary. He denies it, but I know something is going on, there's just too much evidence."

Anita's smile disappeared and was replaced with a look of grief. She took a tissue and dabbed the corner of her eye.

"Dutton, that's my husband, has been through so much lately. He's under a lot of pressure at work, things have been tight financially, and his mother died last year. He was really close to her and I think it was really hard on him."

Anita told of her suspicions of her husband's infidelity, but then came back to the subject of his mother again.

"If I didn't know better, I'd say his infatuation with his secretary began right after his mother died. It's like he needed something to fill a hole in his life. I always liked his mother. She was a nice lady, but I always had the feeling that Dutton was more connected to her than he was to me. Is that crazy?" she asked quizzically. "To be jealous of your mother-in-law?"

I encouraged Anita to tell me more about Dutton's family.

"Other than his father," she continued, "he believes his family is great. That's because of his mother of course. She was a real saint. His father was extremely harsh with the kids. Their mom was the one they turned to for nurturing. She was really good at listening and being there for them."

Anita seemed relieved to be able to talk about something besides her suspicions of her husband.

"Before she died, Dutton paid for them to get carpet in their house and bought them two nice reclining chairs because he knew his father never would. He used to drive her places because he knew his father wouldn't. He treated his mother real special–I think to make up for what she had to go through living with his dad. One time I was angry at him, and I accused him of treating his mother better than he treated me. He blew up." Anita made an explosion gesture with her arms. "He told me to never say that again. He didn't talk to me for two weeks after that. I learned not to bring up that subject."

Anita paused for moment. "Do you think there could be any connection between his mom dying and him having an affair? They loved each other so much. Maybe his secretary fills that void. Does that sound crazy to you?"

## Nice Guys Tend To Seek The Approval Of Women

Due to their family and social conditioning, Nice Guys tend to seek the approval of women. Even as they are trying to become what they believe women want them to be and doing what they believe women want them to do, Nice Guys tend to experience tremendous frustration in gaining the approval they so intensely desire.

This frustration is due to the reality that, in general, women view men who try to please them as weak and hold these men in contempt. Most women do not want a man who tries to please them—they want a man who knows how to please himself. Women consistently share with me that they don't want a passive, pleasing wimp. *They want a man*—someone with his balls still intact.

## Getting Your Testicles Back

Avoiding relationships with men and seeking the approval of women prevents Nice Guys from getting what they really want in love and life. In order to reverse the effects of the Nice Guy Syndrome, Nice Guys have to reclaim their masculinity. The process involves believing that it really is a good thing to be a man and embracing all of their masculine traits. Reclaiming one's masculinity involves:

- Connecting with other men
- Getting strong

- Finding healthy male role models
- Reexamining one's relationship with one's father

## Connecting With Men Helps Nice Guys Reclaim Their Masculinity

Connecting with men is essential for reclaiming masculinity. Building relationships with men requires a conscious effort. This process begins with a commitment to develop male friendships. In order to do this, recovering Nice Guys must be willing to make the time, take risks, and be vulnerable. For most Nice Guys, time seems to be a big factor that keeps them disconnected from men. It takes time to talk with a neighbor, call up a friend, or go to a ballgame. Since many Nice Guys are enmeshed with their wives, families, or work, this means taking time away from these things.

Connecting with men involves doing guy things with guys. There is no right way to do this, but it can include joining a team, going to sporting events, joining a prayer or discussion group, having a poker night, doing volunteer work, going fishing, going for a run, or just hanging out.

Alan is an example of what can happen when a recovering Nice Guy makes the decision to connect with men. Alan had a difficult time doing things for himself, especially with other men. When he made a conscious effort to begin addressing this issue, he had to first take a look at what kept him disconnected from men, and what he could do to start changing the pattern.

One of the first things Alan did was to join a men's therapy group. Even then, it took more than a year before he began doing things with the men outside of the group. As he did, these men were able to give him feedback about his defense mechanisms that kept him isolated. These men also supported him in changing the ways he related to his wife.

Alan also joined a health club where he started playing volleyball and racquetball with other men. Later, he took the lead in starting up a softball team. At first it was difficult to take time out just for himself, especially when it meant being away from his family.

It took a few years, but Alan now has a couple of close male friends as well as several other guys he sees on a regular basis. He even takes a yearly road trip with friends across the country for a weekend of golf. He looks at these trips with the guys as one of the highlights of his year.

Both Alan and his wife Marie believe Alan's conscious decision to connect with men saved their marriage. Alan had made his wife his emotional center. His life revolved around trying to please her and make her happy. Due to his ineffective covert contracts, Alan never believed Marie gave as much to him as he gave to her. As a result, he was often resentful and passive-aggressive. When Alan began to get his emotional and social needs met with men, it took a lot of pressure off his wife.

As Alan reclaimed his masculine energy, he also began to look more attractive to Marie. Even though it was initially difficult to tell her that he was going to spend time with his friends, she respected him when he did. This newfound respect rekindled the feelings she first felt toward Alan early in their relationship.

As Alan found out, there are numerous benefits from developing male relationships. Perhaps one of the most significant benefits for Nice Guys is that it improves their relationships with women. I consistently tell Nice Guys, "The best thing you can do for your relationship with your girlfriend or wife is to have male friends." As they get many of their emotional needs met with men, recovering Nice Guys become less dependent, needy, manipulative and resentful in their relationships with women.

Developing male relationships makes recovering Nice Guys less susceptible to seeking women's approval, or allowing themselves to be defined by the opposite sex. If the Nice Guy's girlfriend or wife is angry at him or thinks he is a jerk, he can take comfort in knowing his buddies think he is OK. He is therefore less likely to resort to peacekeeping or fixing to try and keep his partner happy.

Friendships with men have the potential for tremendous depth and intimacy because there is no sexual agenda. A Nice Guy will frequently avoid doing anything that might upset his partner and cause her to not want to have sex with him. With men, recovering Nice Guys don't feel like they have to please, placate, lie, caretake or sacrifice like they believe they have to do with women. Not having a sexual agenda removes the fear and dysfunctional dances so common for Nice Guys in their relationships with the opposite sex.

## Breaking The Monogamous Bond To Mom

Developing male relationships helps undo a Nice Guy's monogamous bond with his mother. Little boys get pulled into unhealthy relationships with their mothers only when their fathers allow it. The solution to reversing this dynamic is creating healthy relationships with men.

When my daughter Jamie was 18, she had a boyfriend who had been conditioned to be monogamous to his mother. The boy's father frequently traveled for his job, was emotionally unavailable, rigid, and demanding. The boy's mother smothered her son and made him her emotional partner.

On several occasions, Jamie felt as if she were competing with her boyfriend's mother for his attention and affection. Unfortunately, since the mother had first dibs on him, she usually won. It felt strange to Jamie to be jealous of, and in competition with her boyfriend's mother. Nevertheless, she passed the situation off as just a case of her boyfriend and his mother having a very "close" relationship.

One Friday night, Jamie and I went out for dinner. While we ate, she shared her frustration of having to compete with her boyfriend's mother, especially now that he had joined the Marines and was away at boot camp. I empathized with my daughter and shared the facts of life with her.

"Your boyfriend is a classic Nice Guy," I told her. "He has been conditioned to be monogamous to his mother. Unfortunately, that means that he will never really be able to bond completely with you. Something will always get in the way. You may be tempted to focus on that thing, as if it is the problem. But the real problem is his relationship with his mother."

Jamie wasn't thrilled with what I told her, but for an 18-year-old she was pretty intuitive and knew what I was saying was true. She even shared a few examples of the ways she had already seen this happen.

"Is there any hope?" Jamie asked. "Can he ever break free from his mother and become available for me?"

"Yes," I said. "There is one hope. He has to learn to connect with men in ways that he couldn't with his father." I told her, "I think it is a good thing that he is in the Marines and connecting with men. You can support that too. If you two continue dating or even marry, encourage his relationships with men. They are the one hope you have of him breaking his monogamous bond with his mother."

A month or so later, Jamie flew down to San Diego with her boyfriend's parents to attend his graduation from boot camp. As usual, his mother acted possessive and territorial. Amazingly, Jamie noticed a difference in her boyfriend. On several occasions, he set boundaries with his mother and refused to let her hook an emotional hose up to him. Jamie could tell that this was primarily the result of her boyfriend having bonded with several guys in boot camp, and from embracing his own masculinity.

List three men whom you would like to get to know better. Next to each man's name list a possible activity you could do together. Next to this, write down a date and make a commitment to contact him by this day.

## Getting Strong Helps Nice Guys
## Reclaim Their Masculinity

Masculinity denotes strength and power. Because of their conditioning, Nice Guys tend to fear these traits. As a result, they often become emotionally and physically soft. Some even take pride in this softness. I've met many Nice Guys who work out or practice martial arts, but who are still afraid of their strength.

Embracing one's masculinity means embracing one's body, power, and spaciousness. In order to do this, recovering Nice Guys have to stop putting junk into their bodies and train them to respond to the physical demands of being male. This involves eating healthy foods, eliminating drugs and alcohol, working out, drinking lots of water, playing, relaxing, and getting enough rest. Whether the Nice Guy stays fit by running, swimming, weight training, martial arts, playing basketball, volleyball, or tennis, this physical strength translates into self-confidence and power in every other aspect of his life.

Travis, an attorney in his early fifties, is a good example. Travis came to see me to deal with his marital difficulties. During the first session of counseling, two things became immediately evident: First, Travis was a Nice Guy, and second, he had a drug and alcohol problem. I told him I would work with him only if he got a drug and alcohol assessment, quit drinking, and started attending Alcoholics Anonymous. Travis complied with all my boundaries and asked if he could join one of the No More Mr. Nice Guy groups.

Over the next several months, Travis's relationship with his wife was up and down like a yo-yo. In addition to marital problems, it also became apparent that Travis had a number of other lifestyle problems. His diet consisted primarily of fast food. He was a chain smoker and he drank several cups of coffee a day. He worked long hours and got absolutely no exercise.

Over the next several months, Travis began to address these issues one at a time. He started taking time away from work to attend AA meetings and spend time with other recovering men. He decided to have a surgery he had been putting off for years. Since he wouldn't be able to smoke for a few days, he decided it was a good time to quit for good. After his surgery, he began going for walks during his lunch hour. He started drinking more water and cut back on his coffee and soft drink consumption. He even took a week off from work and went fishing with some friends in Alaska.

About 10 months after joining the Nice Guy group, he shared that he was filing for divorce. With his lifestyle changes and the support of the group he had come to realize that his combative relationship with his wife was his last bad habit that needed to go. While relaying his decision to the group, he revealed that his wife blamed the group for killing their marriage. Travis smiled and then wiped a tear from the corner of his eye. "Thanks to this group, I feel strong. I never could have made these changes without your help. This group didn't kill my marriage. It saved my life."

---

**BREAKING FREE:**
# ACTIVITY
## 26

Identify three ways in which you neglect your body. Write down three ways in which you can start taking better care of yourself.

---

## Seeking Out Healthy Role Models Helps
## Nice Guys Reclaim Their Masculinity

I encourage recovering Nice Guys to visualize what they think a healthy male would look like, and think of healthy masculine traits they would like to develop. With that picture in mind, they can go out and look for men who have these kinds of qualities. These men may be in their church, their company, their softball team, even characters on TV or the movies. By observing how these men live their lives and interact with the world, the Nice Guy can begin assimilating a healthier model of manhood.

Like many recovering Nice Guys, I have done this work by committee. I developed a friendship with one man who was good at doing guy things. I formed a relationship with another guy who was a hard worker. I created a relationship with a man who was comfortable revealing himself and sharing his feelings. I made another friend who was good at taking risks and challenging himself. Each of these men in their own way helped me see what it looks like to be male, and have been role models for reclaiming my own masculinity.

---

**BREAKING FREE:**
# ACTIVITY
## 27

Visualize what you think a healthy male would look like. What personality traits would he possess? Write these down. Do you know anyone who has a number of these traits? How could you use this person as a healthy role model?

---

## Re-examining Their Relationship With Their Father Helps
## Nice Guys Reclaim Their Masculinity

As I've mentioned before, most Nice Guys do not report having had a close relationship with their father in childhood. Their fathers were either passive, unavailable, absent, or defined in some negative way. Reclaiming their masculinity requires that Nice Guys examine their relationships with their fathers and take a look at them through adult eyes.

Matthew, a computer programmer in his mid forties is a good example of this process. On one occasion in a No More Mr. Nice Guy group, Matthew stated that he had no intention of attending his father's funeral when he should die. Months later, after exploring his relationship with his father in the group, he decided to call and confront his dad when he didn't get invited to a family function.

Matt's mother had always portrayed his dad as a villain while representing herself as a victim. While talking with his father, Matthew came to the realization that even though his dad had problems, he wasn't bad like his mother had made him out to be. From this encounter, Matthew also realized that he had created a similar scenario with his wife, identifying her as the villain and himself as the victim. Not only did that phone call to his father begin to change his relationship with his dad, but also with his wife.

For Nice Guys, re-examining their relationship with their fathers means seeing their dads through their own eyes as they really are. It means taking them out of the gutter or off the pedestal. This may require that Nice Guys hold them accountable by expressing their feelings to them—including rage and anger. This is essential, even if these men are dead. Sometimes this takes place in their fathers' presence, sometimes not. It's not so important that the father is available to do this work. What is essential is that recovering Nice Guys embrace the male heritage they and their fathers share.

The goal is to find a way to view fathers more accurately. Recovering Nice Guys can begin to accept these men for who they were and are—wounded human beings. This shift is essential if Nice Guys are going to view themselves more accurately, accept themselves for who they are, and reclaim their masculinity.

Embracing masculinity involves coming to see Dad more accurately. To facilitate this process, create a list. On the left side, list a number of your father's characteristics. Write the opposite characteristic on the right side. Indicate where on the spectrum between the two that you see yourself.

When recovering Nice Guys do this exercise they are often surprised at what they discover about their fathers and themselves.

They often see how they have made their fathers into a caricature–a distortion of who they really are.

They may realize that if the man they have become is based on a reaction to how they saw their fathers, they too have become caricatures. Remember, the opposite of crazy is still crazy.

They realize that if their lives are a reaction to dad, then dad is still in control.

They discover that they can be different from dad without being the opposite.

They often come to realize that they have more traits in common with their fathers than they had previously realized or wanted to accept.

## Passing The Benefits of Masculinity On To The Next Generation Part 1: Snakes And Snails

As I work to raise my sons, I realize that they are growing up in a world very much like the one that created my generation of Nice Guys. Boys are disconnected from men and are dependent on gaining the approval of women.

This was brought home to me a couple of years back when our family moved to a new home the summer before my son Steve entered the fourth grade. When I attended his PTA open house, I was jolted with a dose of reality. In kindergarten through fifth grade, there was only one male classroom teacher in the whole school. That's about a

20-to-1 ratio. As the teachers were introduced a grade at a time and then stood together on the gym floor, I received a visual picture of the environment in which little boys spend the most impressionable years of their lives.

As a recovering Nice Guy, I have a unique chance to pass on a new model of masculinity, not only to my sons and daughter, but to a whole generation of boys and girls. The more time I spend working with Nice Guys, the more I realize that this process represents a powerful tool for giving the next generation a saner model of what it means to be men and women.

Unfortunately, our culture provides few rituals in which adult-males help boys leave the comfort of a nursery ruled by women (home, preschool, school) and enter the world of adult manhood. Robert Bly discusses the importance of these rituals in his book *Iron John.*

In "primitive" societies, Bly writes, the boys are pretty much raised by the women until early adolescence. When it is time for the boys to leave the sphere of female influence and move into the men's world, the men of the tribe stage a raid. They put on their war paint, enter the village, and steal the boys away. The women, on cue, weep, protest, and do their best to hang onto the boys. After the men have taken the boys outside the village for their period of initiation, the women get together and ask, "How did I do? Was I believable?" In these cultures, the men and women work together to facilitate this process of transition and initiation.

These days, boys try to make this transition from a world ruled by women, but they can't do it on their own. I have a theory that the phase that adolescent boys pass through where they dress sloppily, look scraggly, act aggressively, hole up in their room, slouch, play loud music, swear, and spit a lot, are all unconsciously aimed at making themselves so repulsive that even their mothers can't stand them. This helps them break the symbiotic bonds with their moms.

Nevertheless, these young men still need help from adult males in pulling away from their mothers without feeling guilt and shame and without overly self-destructive behaviors.

I believe recovering Nice Guys can help boys find a saner model of what it means to be male in our culture. This is because there are certain things that boys can only learn from men. As Nice Guys embrace their masculinity, they can teach their sons what it means to be male. This includes how to handle their aggression, how to handle their libido, how to relate to women, how to bond with a man, and, perhaps most importantly, how to embrace their own masculinity. Men teach these lessons both by example and by interaction with young boys.

As a recovering Nice Guy, I also benefit from being with my adolescent sons and their friends. When I'm around my boys, I get to see unbridled maleness in action. Not only do I get to teach my sons how to handle their testosterone-related behaviors, such as aggression and sexuality, they also show me how to embrace mine.

This reciprocal process requires time and interaction. Fathers need to take their sons hunting and fishing, work on cars with them, take them to work, coach their teams, take them to ball games, work out with them, take them on business trips, and let them tag along with them when they go out with the guys. All of these activities help boys move successfully into the male world.

This process is not just limited to a man's biological sons. Nice Guys can get involved with young relatives, scouts, sports teams, school activities, or big brothers.

Trey, a single man in his late thirties, illustrates the power of this male influence. One night in his men's group, Trey talked about his nephew who was being raised by Trey's sister, a single mother. Trey had strong feelings about what was happening to his nephew because the boy was going through some of the same rebellion and acting out with alcohol that Trey had experienced at the same age. The group encouraged Trey to reach out to his nephew and be a positive male influence.

The next week in group, Try was beaming. He told how he had taken his nephew to the hardware store, and how the two of them had put together a workbench. His nephew was thrilled with the male contact. Trey came away with a feeling that he had done something positive to help change the direction of a struggling young boy.

---

**BREAKING FREE:**
# ACTIVITY
## 29

How can you provide a healthy male support system for the boys and young men you know? List three boys along with an activity you can participate in with them.

---

## Passing The Benefits On Part 2:
## Sugar And Spice

Little girls can benefit from this reclaimed masculine energy as well. The men in one of my No More Mr. Nice Guy groups showed me the benefits of male energy on a young girl in a powerful way. One of the members, LeMar, had a 12-year-old daughter with bone cancer. She had to have a leg removed and undergo chemotherapy and radiation. As a result, she had spent countless days and nights in a hospital bed. One Friday evening, while LeMar was sitting at the hospital at his daughter's bedside, the members of his men's group showed up unexpectedly to take him out to dinner.

In addition to providing masculine support for LeMar during a difficult time, the men also produced an unexpected dividend. Energized by their presence, LeMar's daughter sat up and received hugs from each guy. That night she needed less medication and slept better than she had in weeks. The next day, all she could talk about was "her guys" who had come to visit her the night before.

Recovering Nice Guys can show their daughters what a real man looks like. Girls benefit by seeing their fathers set boundaries, ask for what they want in clear and direct ways, work hard, create, produce, have male friends, and make their own needs a priority. As with little boys, girls can learn what it means to be male both by watching their fathers and by interacting with them. This modeling will have a positive influence on their choice of future partners.

## A No-Lose Situation

As Nice Guys reclaim their masculine energy, everyone wins. Not only does the recovering Nice Guy get to experience deeper bonds with men, but his relationships with women grow too. Perhaps most significantly, a whole new generation of boys and girls reap the benefits of seeing what a healthy male really looks like.

# SEVEN

# GET THE LOVE YOU WANT: SUCCESS STRATEGIES FOR INTIMATE RELATIONSHIPS

## "I'M A VICTIM OF HER DYSFUNCTION."

Karl, a successful businessman in his mid thirties, began his first counseling session with the preceding analysis of his relationship with his wife Danita. Though over six-foot-two and professionally dressed in a dark suit and tie, Karl looked like a little boy sitting on the sofa in my office. Karl's frustration and helplessness regarding his most intimate relationship was unmistakable.

As Karl continued to talk about his marriage, it became apparent that he was intimidated by his wife Danita. He claimed she was "angry all the time." When talking about her he used adjectives like "relentless" and "steamroller." Because of his fear of her anger, he lied to her and avoided interacting with her.

"In many ways," Karl revealed, "Danita is just like my mother. There was just no pleasing Mom. I learned to just avoid her and tune her out when she was bitching. I got really good at lying and hiding what I didn't want her to know about. I guess I'm still pretty good at that today."

As Karl brought the discussion back to the present, he revealed, "Every other area of my life is great. If it wasn't for Danita, my life would be perfect. I just don't think she knows how to be happy."

## Intimate Strangers

In general, Nice Guys end up in my office for one of two reasons. Sometimes some hidden behavior—an affair, surfing for pornography on the Internet, smoking pot—has blown up in their face and created a crisis with their wife or girlfriend. More often, their call to a therapist is motivated by some problem or dissatisfaction in their most intimate relationship; their partner doesn't want to have sex as often as they do, she is depressed, angry, unavailable, or unfaithful (or all of the above).

These men usually believe there is a simple answer to their problem. Some of them are sure everything will be OK if they can just stop doing that one thing that keeps making their partner so angry. The rest of them are convinced that if they can get their partner to change, then life will be great.

A note: *The majority of the men with whom I work are heterosexual. Though I have observed similar relationship issues with gay men, many of the examples I use in this chapter reflect male/female relationships. More often than not, I will use the pronoun "she" or "her" when referring to the Nice Guy's partner.*

Intimate relationships are often an area of great frustration and bewilderment for Nice Guys. Most Nice Guys profess a great desire for intimacy and happiness with their significant other. Nevertheless, intimacy represents an enigmatic riddle for the majority of these men.

Here is what I have concluded after several years of observing countless Nice Guys:

*Even though Nice Guys often profess a deep desire to be intimately con-*
*nected with another individual, their internalized toxic shame and childhood*
*survival mechanisms make such connections difficult and problematic.*

## Why Nice Guys Struggle To Get
## The Love They Want

There are a number of reasons why Nice Guys have difficulty getting
the love they want. These include:

- Their toxic shame
- The dysfunctional relationships they co-create
- Their patterns of enmeshment and avoidance
- The familiar childhood relationship dynamics they recreate
- Their unconscious need to remain monogamous to
  their mother
- They are "bad enders"

## Toxic Shame Prevents Nice Guys From
## Getting The Love They Want

Intimacy implies vulnerability. I define intimacy as "knowing the self,
being known by another, and knowing another." Intimacy requires
two people who are willing to courageously look inward and make
themselves totally visible to another. Internalized toxic shame makes
this kind of exposure feel life-threatening for Nice Guys.

Intimacy, by its nature, would require the Nice Guy to look into
the abyss of his most inner self and allow others to peer into these
same places. It would require the Nice Guy to let someone get close
enough to see into all the nooks and crannies of his soul. This ter-
rifies Nice Guys, because being known means being found out. All
Nice Guys have worked their entire lives to become what they believe
others want them to be while trying to hide their perceived flaws. The
demands of intimacy represent everything Nice Guys fear most.

## Co-creating Dysfunctional Relationships Prevents
## Nice Guys From Getting The Love They Want

The Nice Guy's ongoing attempt to hide his perceived badness makes intimacy a challenge. The moment a Nice Guy enters a relationship he begins a balancing act. In relationships, a life-and-death struggle is played out to balance their fear of vulnerability with their fear of isolation. Vulnerability means someone may get too close to them and see how bad they are. Nice Guys are convinced that when others make this discovery, these people will hurt them, shame them, or leave them.

The alternative doesn't seem any better. Isolating themselves from others re-creates the abandonment experiences that were so terrifying in childhood.

In order to balance his fear of vulnerability and fear of abandonment, a Nice Guy needs help. He finds it in people who are equally wounded and also have difficulty with intimacy. Together they cocreate relationships that simultaneously frustrate all parties while protecting them from their fear of being found out.

Even though it may look like many of the problems Nice Guys experience in relationships are caused by the baggage their partner brings with them, this is not the case. It is the relationship the Nice Guy and his partner cocreate that is the problem.

It is true that Nice Guys often pick partners who appear to be projects, and indeed, they do at times pick some pretty messed up people. The fact that these partners may have challenges—they are single moms, they have financial problems, they are angry, addictive, depressed, overweight, non-sexual, or unable to be faithful—is precisely the reason Nice Guys invite these people into their lives. As long as attention is focused on the flaws of the partner, it is diverted away from the internalized toxic shame of the Nice Guy. This balancing act ensures that the Nice Guy's closest relationship will most likely be his least intimate.

## Patterns Of Enmeshment And Avoidance Prevent Nice Guys From Getting The Love They Want

This intimacy balancing act gets played out in two distinct ways for Nice Guys. The first is through becoming overly involved in an intimate relationship at the expense of one's self and other outside interests. The second is through being emotionally unavailable to a primary partner while playing the Nice Guy role outside of the relationship. I call the first type of Nice Guy an *enmesher* and the second type an *avoider.*

The enmeshing Nice Guy makes his partner his emotional center. His world revolves around her. She is more important than his work, his buddies, his hobbies. He will do whatever it takes to make her happy. He will give her gifts, try to fix her problems, and arrange his schedule to be with her. He will gladly sacrifice his wants and needs to win her love. He will even tolerate her bad moods, rage attacks, addictions, and emotional or sexual unavailability—all because he "loves her so much."

I sometimes refer to enmeshing Nice Guys as *table dogs.* They are like little dogs who stand beneath the table just in case a scrap happens to fall their way. Enmeshing Nice Guys do this same hovering routine around their partner just in case she happens to drop him a scrap of sexual interest, a scrap of her time, a scrap of a good mood, or a scrap of her attention. Even though they are settling for the leftovers that fall from the table, enmeshing Nice Guys think they are getting something really good.

On the surface it may appear that the enmeshing Nice Guy desires, and is available for, an intimate relationship, but this is an illusion. The Nice Guy's pursuing and enmeshing behavior is an attempt to hook up an emotional hose to his partner. This hose is used to suck the life out of her and fill an empty place inside of him. The Nice Guy's partner unconsciously picks up on this agenda and works like hell to make sure the Nice Guy can't get close enough to hook up the hose. Consequently, the Nice Guy's partner is often seen as the one preventing the closeness the Nice Guy desires.

The avoider can be a little tougher to get a handle on. *The avoiding Nice Guy seems to put his job, hobby, parents, and everything else before his primary relationship.* He may not seem like a Nice Guy to his partner at all because he is often nice to everyone else but her. He may volunteer to work on other people's cars. He may spend weekends fixing his mother's roof. He may work two or three jobs. He may volunteer to work on other people's cars. He may spend weekends fixing his mother's roof. He may work two or three jobs. He may coach his children's sports teams. Even though he may not follow his partner around and cater to her every whim, he still operates from a covert contract that since he is a Nice Guy, his partner should be available to him, even if he isn't available to her.

Both patterns, enmeshing and avoiding, inhibit any real kind of intimacy from occurring. They may help the Nice Guy feel safe, but they won't help him feel loved.

---

**BREAKING FREE:**
# ACTIVITY
## 30

Ask yourself: are you an enmesher or an avoider in your present relationship? How would your partner see you? Does the pattern ever change? What roles have you played in past relationships?

---

## Re-creating Familiar Childhood Relationship Patterns Prevents Nice Guys From Getting The Love They Want

It is human nature to be attracted to what is familiar. Because of this reality, Nice Guys create adult relationships that mirror the dynamics of their dysfunctional childhood relationships. For example:

If listening to his mother's problems as a child gave a Nice Guy a sense of connection, he may grow up believing such behavior equals intimacy. In order to feel valuable and connected in his adult relationships, he will have to pick a partner who has her fair share of problems.

If he was trained to caretake and fix needy or dependent family members, the Nice Guy may find a way to do the same in his adult relationships.

If he believes he can only get his own needs met after he had met the needs of other more important people, the Nice Guy may sacrifice himself for the sake of his partner.

If he was abandoned in childhood, he may choose partners who are unavailable or unfaithful.

If he grew up with an angry, demeaning, or controlling parent, he may choose a partner with similar traits.

Occasionally, the person the Nice Guy chooses to help him recreate his childhood relationship patterns isn't the way he unconsciously needs her to be when the relationship begins. If this is the case, he will often help her become what he needs. He may project upon her one or more traits of his parents. He may act as if she is a certain way, even when she isn't. His unconscious dysfunctional needs may literally force his partner to respond in an equally dysfunctional way.

For example, as a child I never knew what kind of mood my father would be in when I came into the house. More often than not, it wasn't good. I learned to come home prepared for the worst. I later recreated the same pattern in my marriage. I projected my father's unpredictable moods onto my wife and would frequently arrive home prepared for her to be angry. Even if she was in a good mood, my defensiveness often triggered some kind of confrontation between us. Thus Elizabeth came to look like my angry father and I perpetuated a familiar, though dysfunctional relationship dynamic.

We tend to be attracted to people who have some of the worst traits of both of our parents. Instead of blaming your partner for your unconscious choice, identify the ways in which she helps you recreate familiar relationship patterns from your childhood. Share this with your partner.

## The Unconscious Need To Remain Monogamous To Mom Prevents Nice Guys From Getting The Love They Want

The tendency of Nice Guys to be monogamous to their mothers seriously inhibits having a genuinely intimate relationship with a partner in adulthood. Nice Guys are creative in finding ways to maintain this childhood bond. What all of these behaviors have in common is that they all effectively insure that the Nice Guy will not be able to bond in any significant way with any woman except his mother.

The following are a few of the ways Nice Guys unconsciously maintain a monogamous bond to their mothers. Look over the list. Note any of the behavior patterns that may serve to keep you monogamous to your mother. Share this information with a safe person.

- Over-involvement with work or hobbies
- Creating relationships with people who need fixing
- Addictions to drugs or alcohol
- Sexual addictions to pornography, masturbation, fantasy, chat lines, or hookers
- Affairs

- Sexual dysfunction—lack of desire, inability to get or maintain an erection, or premature ejaculation
- Forming relationships with women who are angry, sick, depressive, compulsive, addicted, unfaithful, or otherwise unavailable
- Avoiding intercourse or taking vows of celibacy

---

## Being Bad Enders Prevents Nice Guys From Getting The Love They Want

Finally, Nice Guys have difficulty getting the love they want because they spend too much time trying to make bad relationships work. Basically, Nice Guys suffer from the age-old problem of looking for love in all the wrong places. If a Nice Guy spends all of his time stuck in a bad relationship, it pretty much guarantees he won't find one that might work better.

When healthy individuals recognize that they have created a relationship that is not a good fit, or that a partner they have chosen lacks the basic qualities they desire, they move on. Not Nice Guys. Due to their conditioning, Nice Guys just keep trying harder to get a non-workable situation to work or get someone to be something they are not. This tendency frustrates everybody involved.

Even when Nice Guys do try to end a relationship, they are not very good at it. They frequently do it too late and in indirect, blaming, or deceitful ways. They typically have to do it several times before it sticks. I often joke that, on average, it takes Nice Guys about nine attempts to end a relationship. (Unfortunately, this isn't far from the truth.)

## Strategies For Building Successful Relationships

There are no perfect relationships. There are no perfect partners. Relationships by their very nature are chaotic, eventful, and challenging. The second part of this chapter is not a plan for finding a perfect partner or creating the perfect relationship. It is simply a strategy for doing what works. By adapting the points below and changing the way in which they live their lives, recovering Nice Guys will change the way they have relationships. Nice Guys can:

- Approve of themselves
- Put themselves first
- Reveal themselves to safe people
- Eliminate covert contracts
- Take responsibility for their own needs
- Surrender
- Dwell in reality
- Express their feelings
- Develop integrity
- Set boundaries
- Embrace their masculinity

Previous chapters have included illustrations of what can happen to relationships when Nice Guys begin to make these life changes. Let's examine a little more closely how applying a couple of these life strategies can help recovering Nice Guys get the love they want.

---

### A WARNING

If you are in a relationship, the program of recovery from the Nice Guy Syndrome presented in this book will seriously affect you and your partner. One of two things will happen:

1) Your present relationship will begin to grow and evolve in exciting and unpredictable ways.

2) Your present relationship will be sent to a long overdue grave.

---

# Learning To Approve Of Themselves
# Helps Nice Guys Get The Love They Want

The essence of recovery from the Nice Guy Syndrome is the conscious decision to live one's life just as one desires. I frequently encourage recovering Nice Guys to be just who they are, without reservation. I support them in deciding what is right for them and being that with all of their energy for the whole world to see. The people who like them just as they are will hang around. The people who don't, won't. This is the only way to have a healthy relationship. No one really wants to believe that they have to be false or hide who they really are to get someone to love them or stay with them. Yet, this is a common dynamic in the intimate relationships Nice Guys create.

George is a good example of what can happen when a recovering Nice Guy decides to start pleasing himself and stop pleasing his partner.

Throughout his relationship with his wife Susan, George's primary goal was to make her happy. Over a period of five years, George gave up hunting and fishing (two of his passions), quit hanging out with his friends, turned the control of his finances over to Susan, and supported her in quitting her job because she was unhappy at work. These changes occurred gradually. All were an attempt on George's part to please Susan.

Nevertheless, Susan was rarely happy. By the time George joined a No More Mr. Nice Guy group, he felt helpless and resentful and was ready to leave his wife. George saw Susan as the cause of the frustration he was feeling. George spent the first few weeks in our group complaining about his wife. Eventually, the group members began to confront George on his victim role and challenged him to do something different instead of blaming Susan.

It took a few more months, but George began to change. The most significant change was a conscious decision to quit trying to make Susan happy. He realized that his attempts to please her weren't working and were causing him to feel resentful.

George began by setting aside one weekend a month to go hunting or fishing. When Susan tried several different methods to manipulate him or guilt him out of his decision, he held fast. Next, instead of handing his paycheck over to Susan to control, he began giving himself an allowance to spend how he wanted. This too drew resistance from his wife. Perhaps the most frightening step was when George set up a budget and told Susan that if she wanted more control over the income, she would have to go back to working full time.

Ironically, two things began to happen. George felt less like a victim and actually started having more positive feelings toward Susan. Second, Susan began taking charge of her own life and became less dependent on George. After about a year in the group, George shared how much more content he was and how much his marriage had improved. He gave credit to the group members who supported him in finding the courage to start pleasing himself and stop trying to make Susan happy.

---

### BREAKING FREE:
# ACTIVITY
### 33

List some of the ways you try to please your partner. What changes would you make if you did not have to worry about making her happy?

---

## Setting Boundaries Helps Nice Guys Get The Love They Want

The subject of boundaries was presented in Chapter Five. Nowhere is the issue of boundary setting more important for Nice Guys than in their most intimate relationships. By setting healthy boundaries with their partners, Nice Guys create situations in which both they and their partner can feel safe to be vulnerable and experience true intimacy.

I show Nice Guys, often with their partners watching, how to step up to their line and set boundaries. On more than one occasion, I have had the partner of a Nice Guy applaud during the demonstration. The Nice Guy will turn, slack-jawed, and say, "You mean you want me to stand up to you, dear?"

"Of course I do," she will respond. "I don't want to be married to someone I can walk all over."

Then I warn him. "Your wife is telling you the truth. She doesn't feel safe knowing she can push you around. She wants to know that you will stand up to her. That is how she will feel secure in the relationship. But, here's the catch. She has to test to see if she can trust you. The first time you set a boundary with her she may react intensely. She will push against it. She will tell you that you are wrong for setting that boundary. She will do her best to find out if your boundary is for real."

When a recovering Nice Guy sets boundaries with his partner, it makes her feel secure. In general, when women feel secure, they feel loved. She will also come to know that if her partner will stand up to her, he is also likely to stand up for her. Setting boundaries also creates respect. When a Nice Guy fails to set boundaries it communicates to his partner that he doesn't really honor himself, so why should she?

To help Nice Guys decide if they need to set a boundary with a particular behavior, I have them apply the *Second Date Rule.* Using the second date rule, Nice Guys ask themselves, "If this behavior had occurred on the second date, would there have been a third?" This question helps them see if they have been putting up with something that they shouldn't.

When trying to decide how to deal with a behavior they have deemed unacceptable, I encourage Nice Guys to apply the *Healthy*

*Male Rule.* Following this rule of thumb, they simply ask themselves, "How would a healthy male handle this situation?" For some reason, just asking this question connects them with their intuitive wisdom and helps them access the power they need to respond appropriately.

Once the Nice Guy knows he can set a boundary any time he needs to, he can let people move toward him, get close, have feelings, be sexual, and so on. He can let these things happen because he is confident that at any point, if he begins to feel uncomfortable, he can say "stop," "no," or "slow down," or can remove himself. He can do whatever he needs to do to take care of himself.

---

### BREAKING FREE:
# ACTIVITY
## 34

Are there any areas in your personal relationships in which you avoid setting appropriate boundaries? Do you:
- Tolerate intolerable behavior
- Avoid dealing with a situation because it might cause conflict
- Not ask for what you want
- Sacrifice yourself to keep the peace

If you applied the Second Date rule or the Healthy Male rule to these situations, how might you change your behavior?

---

## Additional Strategies For Happy, Healthy Relationships

In addition to the program of recovery presented in previous chapters of *No More Mr. Nice Guy,* there are a few additional strategies that will help Nice Guys get the love they want. These include:

- Focusing on their relationship, not their partner
- Not reinforcing undesirable behaviors
- Doing something different

## Focusing On Their Relationship, Not Their Partner, Helps Nice Guys Get The Love They Want

Wounded people are attracted to wounded people. When Nice Guys enter a relationship, they frequently choose partners who look more dysfunctional than they do. This creates a dangerous illusion that one of them is sicker than the other. This is a distortion, because healthy people are not attracted to unhealthy people—and vice versa. I frequently tell couples that if you have one obviously wounded person in a relationship, you always have two. No exception.

When my wife Elizabeth and I first got together, we created a system in which she was identified as the broken one while I was designated the healthy one. These scripts worked well for both of us until she started going to counseling. One day, she came home from a therapy session and announced that she had discovered that I was just as messed up as she was. Because I couldn't entertain the idea that I was "messed up," I responded, "No, you are really finding out that you are just as healthy as I am."

The relationship system we had created together allowed both of us to play familiar, yet dysfunctional roles. Unfortunately, it also prevented any kind of real intimacy until Elizabeth began to challenge the status quo. I've listened to countless Nice Guys who have formed relationships like the one Elizabeth and I initially created. These men have the belief that they are victims to their "sick" partner's dysfunction. This illusion keeps everyone involved stuck in repetitive, ineffective patterns.

By focusing on their relationship instead of their partner, recovering Nice Guys are able to use their partner to get in touch with their childhood experiences of abandonment, neglect, abuse, and smothering. They can use this information to better understand why they have created the kind of relationship system they have. This process enables them to make changes that allow them to get what they want in their intimate relationships.

Instead of saying "if she would just . . . ," the recovering Nice Guy has to ask,

"Why did I need to cocreate this relationship?"

"How does this relationship let me play familiar roles?"

"How does this relationship let me meet unconscious needs?"

"Why did I invite this person into my life?"

When the recovering Nice Guy begins asking these kinds of questions, he can begin to see his significant other as a partner in healing. This not only shifts how he views his partner, but also allows him to address childhood issues that prevent him from having a truly intimate relationship.

In the beginning of this chapter, we met Karl—whose wife Danita seemed as hard to please as his cold, critical mother. Karl never knew when his mom might get angry, criticize, or shame him. In adulthood, Karl cocreated a similar dynamic with Danita. When she got angry, Karl would use all of his childhood survival mechanisms, like avoidance and withdrawal, to try to cope. Karl would accuse Danita of "being angry all the time" and would walk on eggshells to avoid upsetting her. Karl would tell himself, "I don't deserve this." He would then retreat and create escape scenarios in his head.

The relationship began to shift when Karl came to see Danita as a "gift" whom he invited into his life to help him clean out his old issues around his fear of angry and critical people. As Karl made this shift several things began to happen. He began to have grief for what he went through as a child. He began standing up to Danita rather than avoiding and withdrawing. As he came to see Danita's anger as a result of her own childhood wounding, Danita began to look less and less angry to him. As his view of his wife began to shift, Karl began to feel more loving toward Danita and their relationship began to show marked improvement.

The next time you find yourself feeling frustrated, resentful, or rageful at your partner, ask yourself these questions:

"Why have I invited this person into my life?"

"What do I need to learn from this situation?"

"How would my view of this situation change if I saw it as a gift?"

## Not Reinforcing Undesirable Behaviors Helps Nice Guys Get The Love They Want

A couple of years ago we bought a Weimaraner puppy. We decided that if we were going to have a big dog in the house, we should take him to obedience school. One of the first lessons we learned was that we were the ones who needed obedience training. Most dogs that behave badly, we found out, have been conditioned to do so by ignorant or inconsistent owners.

In many ways, humans aren't much different from pets. People often behave the way they have been trained to behave. For example, if a person gives his dog a treat when he pisses on the carpet, the dog will keep pissing on the carpet. The same is true for humans. If the Nice Guy reinforces his partner's undesirable behaviors, she will keep behaving in undesirable ways.

Here is the irony for Nice Guys: Nice Guys like the idea of a smooth and problem-free relationship. Typically, if their partner is unhappy, depressed, angry, or having a problem, they will jump right in and try and fix it or make it better. They believe that by doing so, they will make the problem go away and everything will quickly get back to normal. Unfortunately, this is like giving a dog a treat for pissing on the carpet.

Every time a Nice Guy responds to or pays attention to a behavior he would like to eliminate, he is actually reinforcing that very behavior. This reinforcement increases the likelihood that that behavior will occur again. For example, Joe's wife frequently came home from work in a silent rage over some problem she experienced with a coworker. It bothered Joe when his wife was in this mood. In an attempt to relieve his anxiety, he would ask his wife what was wrong. After a little coaxing, she would spend the next couple of hours venting to Joe about how mistreated she was at work. Joe would listen and offer helpful suggestions, hoping that by doing so, she would get over her mood.

In his attempt for short-term anxiety relief, Joe had actually helped create a long-term problem. Every time he asked his wife what was wrong, listened for hours, and offered advice, he was actually reinforcing a behavior pattern he found undesirable.

In dog obedience school we learned that if you want an undesirable behavior to go away, you stop paying attention to it. The same is true in relationships.

Like many Nice Guys, Joe felt like a victim to his wife's behavior. He was oblivious to the fact that he was responsible for perpetuating a behavior he found undesirable. When the men in his No More Mr. Nice Guy group pointed this fact out to him, he decided to try something different.

The next time his wife came home in a silent, withdrawn mood, he didn't say anything. He ate dinner in silence and then went out to the garage. Even though he felt intense anxiety, he resisted his impulses to try to "fix" his wife. As he lay awake in bed that night, the deafening silence kept him awake for hours. The next morning, the silence continued. Joe was afraid this behavior might go on forever. In an attempt to relieve his anxiety, he tried making a little small talk. His wife responded with one-word answers and left for work.

That evening, it seemed as if a miracle had occurred. Joe's wife came home from work in a good mood and asked Joe if he wanted to go for a walk. While walking she told him how she had resolved the previous day's problem. Joe revealed to his wife how uncomfortable it had made him to not try to fix her problem, the previous evening. She responded by telling Joe that she didn't want him to try to fix her problems and that she liked it better that he had given her some space to work it out on her own.

## Doing Something Different When Beginning A New Relationship Helps Nice Guys Get The Love They Want

For Nice Guys who see a relationship come to an end, or for the ones who are presently single, I encourage them to take a different approach when beginning new relationships. Relationships are messy and there is no way to eliminate the bumps and potholes, but we don't have to make them any more difficult than they already are. This is one area where I strongly encourage Nice Guys to do something different. That is, enter relationships with a healthy agenda, rather than an unconscious, dysfunctional one.

Doing something different means choosing a different kind of partner. A fixer-upper may be a fun challenge when it comes to restoring a car, but it's a terrible way to choose a partner. Nice Guys have a tendency, due to their own insecurities, to pick partners who seem like they need a little polishing. Because they don't know why a healthy or independent person would want them, they settle for a diamond in the rough. They tend to pick partners who have had troubled childhoods, are sexual abuse survivors, have had a string of bad relationships, are depressed, are having money problems, are overweight, or are struggling single moms. Then they go to work operating from a covert contract—fixing, caretaking, and pleasing—all with the hope that she will turn out to be a polished gem. Unfortunately, this strategy rarely works.

When recovering Nice Guys create relationships with people who don't need fixing, they improve their odds of finding the love they want. This doesn't mean searching for the perfect partner, just one who is already taking responsibility for her own life. Over time, the members of my No More Mr. Nice Guy groups have come up with a number of traits to consciously look for when creating new relationships. These traits include (in no particular order):

- Passion
- Integrity
- Happiness
- Intelligence
- Sexual assertiveness
- Financial responsibility.
- Commitment to personal growth.

Nice Guys who are already in a relationship may find it unsettling if their current partner doesn't fare well by this list (especially if it is the Nice Guy doing the evaluating). That doesn't mean they need to jump out of the relationship and go looking for greener pastures. Instead, I encourage these men to first begin addressing their own behaviors and look at why they needed to create the kind of relationship they have with their present partner.

Finding a new partner won't be the solution if the Nice Guy still needs the same kind of relationship. I have found that when recovering Nice Guys begin dealing with their own dysfunctional patterns, their relationships also begin changing. At times these changes cause them to re-evaluate their desire to get out. Sometimes they confirm it is time for a change.

Nice Guys have a strong tendency to try to do everything "right." This list isn't meant as a magic formula. There are no perfect people and no perfect relationships. But by consciously looking for the traits listed above in a prospective partner, Nice Guys can save themselves a lot of grief and improve their chances of actually finding what they are looking for.

Doing something different also means refraining from being sexual in new relationships. Nice Guys must give themselves a chance to accurately evaluate the traits listed above by staying out of bed with a person until they really get to know her. Once the sex begins in relationships, the learning stops. Sex creates such a powerful bond that it is difficult to accurately evaluate the appropriateness of a new relationship. Nice Guys may often be aware of various traits or behaviors they find unacceptable in a new partner, but if they are already having sex, it is difficult to address these issues and even tougher to end the relationship.

## Embrace The Challenge

Recovering Nice Guys *can* have fulfilling, intimate relationships. Life is a challenge and so are relationships. As they implement the recovery strategies presented in this book, recovering Nice Guys put themselves in the position to embrace these challenges and get the love they want.

# EIGHT

# GET THE SEX YOU WANT: SUCCESS STRATEGIES FOR SATISFYING SEX

T ake everything written about Nice Guys in this book—their shame, their sacrifice of self, their approval seeking, their doing the opposite of what works, their indirectness, their caretaking, their covert contracts, their controlling behavior, their fear, their dishonesty, their difficulty receiving, their dysfunctional relationships, their loss of masculine energy. Now put them all in a great big container, shake them up, open the lid, look inside, and you'll have a pretty good view of how Nice Guys do sex.

For Nice Guys, sex is where all of their abandonment experiences, toxic shame, and dysfunctional survival mechanisms are focused and magnified. I believe it is safe to say that every Nice Guy with whom I have ever worked has had some significant problem with sex. These problems are manifested in many ways, but the most common are:

*Not getting enough.* This is by far the most common sexual complaint of Nice Guys. The focus of this problem is frequently directed at a seemingly sexually inhibited or unavailable partner (or the unavailability of women in general).

*Having to settle for less than satisfying sex.* Nice Guys often settle for bad sex, believing that it is better than no sex at all. Again, the blame is often focused on the Nice Guy's partner.

*Sexual dysfunction.* This usually takes form of an inability to get or maintain an erection, or premature ejaculation.

*Sexual repression.* Some Nice Guys claim to have little or no interest in sex. More often than not, these men are actually engaged in some form of sexual activity that they believe is best kept out of sight.

*Compulsive sexual behavior.* This can include compulsive masturbation, addiction to pornography, affairs, peep shows, 900 numbers, cybersex, and prostitution.

When you add all of these dynamics together, you end up with a breed of men who don't have very much sex and/or don't have very much good sex. Even though most Nice Guys have a tendency to focus on factors outside of themselves as the cause of this problem, the opposite is closer to the truth. It is Nice Guys themselves who are masters at making sure that their sex lives are less than satisfying.

## Shame And Fear

The difficulty Nice Guys have with sex can be directly linked to two issues: shame and fear. All Nice Guys have shame and fear about being sexual and about being sexual beings. In my experience, this is probably the most difficult concept for Nice Guys to understand and accept about themselves. This is so important I will say it again: All Nice Guys have shame and fear about being sexual and about being sexual beings.

If you could peel back a Nice Guy's brain and find the part of the unconscious mind that controls sex, here is what you would find:

- Memories of childhood experiences that made him feel like he was bad
- The pain of not getting his needs met in a timely, healthy manner
- The effects of growing up with sexually wounded parents
- The sexual distortions and illusions of a really screwed up society
- The absence of accurate sexual information when it was needed
- The sexual guilt and shame associated with centuries of religious influence
- The effects of covert sexual bonds created by his mother
- The trauma of sexual violations
- The memories of early sexual experiences wrapped in secrecy
- The distorted and unrealistic images of bodies and sex in pornography
- The shame of hidden, compulsive behaviors
- The memories of previous sexual failures or rejections

Every time a Nice Guy has a sexual feeling or is in a sexual situation, he must negotiate through all of this unconscious baggage. Nice Guys find numerous creative ways to avoid or distract themselves from their sexual shame and fear. Unfortunately, these avoidance and distraction mechanisms prevent Nice Guys from having much of anything that resembles a good sex life. These avoidance and distraction mechanisms include:

- Avoiding sexual situations and sexual opportunities
- Trying to be a good lover
- Hiding compulsive sexual behaviors
- Repressing their life energy
- Settling for bad sex

## Avoidance Of Sexual Situations And Sexual Opportunities Prevents Nice Guys From Getting The Sex They Want

As odd as it may sound, Nice Guys find many creative ways to avoid sex. I have coined the term *Vagiphobia* to describe this propensity. Vagiphobia is a syndrome where the penis tries to stay out of vaginas or gets out quickly once it is in. While this survival mechanism may help protect the Nice Guy from having to experience his shame and fear, it also guarantees he won't have very much sex.

Alan could be the vagiphobia poster child. Alan began therapy due to a problematic habit of entering into sexualized relationships outside of his marriage. Some of these trysts became overtly sexual, yet none were ever consummated with intercourse. The problem came to a head after he began a relationship with one of his wife's girlfriends, and his wife found an incriminating note in his coat pocket.

In therapy, Alan revealed that he liked the attention of women. In social situations he always felt more comfortable connecting with women. Over time, it became apparent that due to childhood conditioning—a monogamous bond with his mother, the decision to be different from his father, and the effects of fundamentalist religious teachings—Alan found creative ways to get the attention of women while avoiding putting his penis in their vaginas. (I refer to this common Nice Guy behavior as "flirting without fucking." As long as the Nice Guy doesn't put his penis in a vagina, he can exchange all kinds of sexual energy yet convince himself he hasn't really had sex or hasn't done anything wrong.)

On one occasion, Alan shared an example with his No More Mr. Nice Guy group of this behavior. Alan had been on a business trip, traveling with a coworker, a young woman whom Alan found very attractive. During the trip, they flirted and exchanged sexual innuen-does. One evening, they sat in the bar and talked about their lives. The evening ended with some slow dancing. The next evening after drinks, the woman invited Alan to join her in the hot tub. She showed up in a revealing string bikini. While in the hot tub, she sat on Alan's lap and they kissed passionately. Even though he was very aroused, he turned down her offer to go up to her room because he didn't want to "jeopardize their working relationship."

This story is consistent with Alan's lifelong avoidance of vaginas. Alan had a couple of girlfriends in high school. But whenever the girls got serious and wanted to move beyond petting, Alan felt smothered and broke up.

Alan portrayed his wife as being sexually withdrawn. One factor that contributed to this situation was that Alan would never directly initiate sex. He believed women thought sex was bad, and he was convinced that if he was too direct in letting them know he wanted to have sex, they would think he was bad.

Alan used his frustration over his wife's sexual unavailability to justify his sexualized behavior with other women. Interestingly enough, Alan had a consistent knack of only flirting with women that weren't very likely to be available to consummate a relationship with him. On the rare occasion that he guessed wrong, Alan would find some good reason to not follow through with what he had started.

## Trying To Be A Good Lover Prevents
## Nice Guys From Getting The Sex They Want

It is not unusual for Nice Guys to pride themselves on being good lovers. Being a good lover can be an attachment these men use to feel valuable. It can be a way to convince themselves they are different from other men. It can also be a very effective mechanism for allowing them to have sex while staying distracted from their internalized shame and fear. As long as they are focused on the arousal and pleasure of their partner, Nice Guys can distract themselves from their own toxic shame, feelings of inadequacy, or fear of being smothered. Terrance, a Nice Guy in his midthirties is a good example.

"I've got a problem with premature ejaculation." This was how Terrance introduced himself in his first therapy session. "My first wife left me for another man," he continued without pausing. "That was devastating. The good news is, I met a wonderful, sensual, sexual woman, and we're engaged to get married. There's only one problem. I come too fast. She turns me on so much, I just get too excited."

Terrance went on to describe how hard he worked to please his girlfriend when they made love. Whenever they had sex, Terrance would try to make sure his girlfriend had two or three orgasms by stimulating her orally before he put his penis inside her vagina. He then tried to bring her to one more climax vaginally. Unfortunately, he frequently ejaculated before she had her final orgasm. Terrance was so seemingly selfless that he told his fiancée that he didn't care if he never had an orgasm, as long as she was satisfied.

"Everything is great except this one issue," Terrance claimed. "Her kids love me. Her parents love me. She says she loves everything about me, except she feels like 30 percent is missing. She doesn't seem to want to make love anymore and is talking about postponing the wedding until I can get this thing fixed."

Most of the time, Nice Guys like Terrance are totally unaware of how much they are missing by trying to be great lovers. When Nice Guys set out to be great lovers, they are actually creating a recipe for boring sex. Sex that focuses on trying to please the other guarantees a routine, do-what-worked-last-time kind of experience. Trying to be a great lover pretty much insures that a Nice Guy will not have many passionate, reciprocal, spontaneous, serendipitous, or intimate sexual experiences—hardly a recipe for good sex!

## Hiding Compulsive Sexual Behaviors Prevents Nice Guys From Getting The Sex They Want

Imagine the financial jackpot of inventing a pill to take away loneliness, cure boredom, alleviate feelings of worthlessness, smooth over conflict, create feelings of being loved, relieve stress, and generally solve all personal problems. Nice Guys believe such a drug exists—they call it sex.

Many Nice Guys discovered at an early age that sexual arousal was a good distraction from the isolation, turmoil, unrealistic demands, and abandonment experiences of their childhood. Unfortunately, when Nice Guys bring their sensual security blanket into adulthood, it prevents them from experiencing intimate and fulfilling sex with another individual.

I have found Nice Guys to be prone to hidden, compulsive sexual behavior. I have developed a theory that states, the nicer the guy, the darker the sexual secrets. I find this to be consistently true. Sex is a basic human drive. Because most Nice Guys believe they are bad for being sexual, or believe that other people will think they are bad, sexual impulses have to be kept hidden from view. The Nice Guy's sexuality doesn't go away, it just goes underground. Therefore, the more dependent a man is on external approval, the deeper he is going to have to hide his sexual behavior.

Lyle, a computer programmer in his midforties, provides a poignant example of this connection. Everybody liked Lyle. He was one of those guys who didn't seem to have any rough edges. A devout Christian, Lyle taught Sunday school and was always willing to help anyone in need.

Lyle's life seemed perfect. There was only one hitch—he was secretly addicted to pornography. Growing up in an Evangelical Christian home, he first discovered this drug when he was nine. A loner as a child, Lyle would spend hours in his tree fort looking at pictures of naked women. With his pornography, he never felt alone.

Fifteen years into his marriage, Lyle's habit remained a well-kept secret. Over the years his compulsive behavior expanded to renting adult videos, visiting peep shows and strip bars, and calling 900 numbers. Most recently, his obsession had found flight in cyberspace.

Frequenting sex chat rooms, he carried on a number of sexual relationships with faceless surfers on the Internet.

Periodically during their marriage, Lyle's wife would confront him over their lackluster sex life. She would protest that it just wasn't normal to go months without having sex. Lyle would validate her feelings and assert that he, too, would like more sex. He would then fall back on the excuse that he was usually too tired from work and too stressed with the demands of family life.

Many times throughout his life, Lyle promised himself he would quit visiting his secret sexual world. Time and time again, he would throw out his stash of magazines or swear off the videos and chat rooms. He would breathe a sigh of relief, only to find himself back at it again weeks or months later.

Lyle, like numerous Nice Guys, invested so much time and energy in his hidden, compulsive sexual behavior that there was little left for a real, person-to-person sexual relationship.

## Repressing Their Life Energy Prevents Nice Guys From Getting The Sex They Want

When a boy reaches adolescence, he must begin negotiating the turbulent seas of learning to relate to the opposite sex. If he is to have any hope of securing a girlfriend and someday having sex, he must figure out what it takes to get a female to notice him and approve of him. For some boys this process seems to come fairly easily. If they happen to be good looking, a star athlete, or from an affluent family, attracting females may not be overly difficult for them.

Once you exclude the minority of adolescent males listed above, that leaves the majority of teenage boys who have no clue of what it will take to get a girl to like them. It is at this point that many young men decide that maybe by being "nice" they will stand out from the other guys and might gain the approval of some member of the opposite sex. This decision is especially important if the young man has already been conditioned to believe that he is not OK just as he is.

It is this strategy formed in adolescence—trying to attract a woman and her sexual favor by being nice—that many Nice Guys carry into adulthood. It is not uncommon for Nice Guys to believe that a woman would be lucky to have them while simultaneously wondering why any woman would want them. Because they can't think of any other reason why a woman would be attracted to them or want to have sex with them, Nice Guys hang on to their strategy of "being nice" even when it consistently proves ineffective in getting them the sex they want.

Ironically, trying to be nice robs a man of his life energy. The more a Nice Guy seeks approval and tries to "do it right," the tighter he clamps a lid down on any kind of energy that might actually draw a person to him. This is why I frequently hear Nice Guys lament about women not being attracted to them. The problem is, once they have repressed all of their life energy, there is little about them to get anyone's attention or turn them on.

Women consistently tell me that even though they may be initially drawn to a Nice Guy's pleasing demeanor, over time they find it difficult to get excited about having sex with him. Often the partner feels defective, but it is really not her fault. There is just very little about the Nice Guy persona to flip a switch or arouse a prospective partner. Once again, by doing the opposite of what works, Nice Guys prevent themselves from getting the sex they want.

## Settling For Bad Sex Prevents Nice Guys From Getting The Sex They Want

The wife of a Nice Guy in her late twenties shared with me how her partner would "pester" her for sex. When she would say "no," he would pout and withdraw. When she did consent to being sexual, he would focus on her arousal while she did little to reciprocate. With pithy awareness she revealed, "I could tell him it would really turn me on if he set himself on fire. He would gladly do it and think he was getting good sex because it made me happy."

By settling for bad sex, Nice Guys ensure that they won't get to experience very much good sex. Aaron provides a good example of a pretty common way Nice Guys create bad sex. Let's visit his bedroom and observe a typical sexual scenario between him and his wife Hannah.

Aaron and Hannah haven't had sex in several weeks, a common occurrence in their relationship. Tonight, Aaron is feeling sexual, but instead of telling Hannah that he wants to make love, he goes into a pattern of indirectly trying to arouse her.

Even though Hannah has let Aaron know on several occasions she resents his "pestering," he moves up behind her in bed and begins to rub her back. As he massages her shoulders he momentarily tunes out his resentment over her sexual unavailability. As he slowly moves his hands down to rub her buttocks, he also tunes out that her body is totally unreceptive to his touch. He hopes that by moving slowly and not alarming her by being too overtly sexual, she will get in the mood. This approach has occasionally worked in the past.

By the time he lightly strokes one of her breasts, Aaron is totally unaware of anything going on inside of his own body. By now, he is focused on Hannah's arousal and trying to anticipate how to stimulate her just enough to get her in the mood without doing too much to make her angry.

Finally, because she hasn't rebuffed his advances, he rolls her over and for the next twenty minutes focuses all of his attention on her arousal until she has an orgasm. Since he is disconnected from his own physical arousal, he has a difficult time climaxing himself. To help himself along, he fantasizes about the young secretary at work. When he finally has an orgasm, he immediately shifts his focus back to his wife to check in on her emotional state. Later, as he rolls over and goes to sleep, Aaron feels empty and resentful.

How's your love life? Are you ready to start getting good sex? If so, read on.

## Getting Good Sex

The rest of this chapter presents a strategy for helping recovering Nice Guys experience satisfying sex. The process includes:

- Coming out of the closet
- Taking matters into their own hands
- Saying "no" to bad sex
- Following the example of the bull moose

## Coming Out Of The Closet Helps
## Nice Guys Get The Sex They Want

Internalized shame and fear are the greatest barriers to a satisfying sex life. A man can read all the books he wants on *How To Pick Up Women* or watch all the instructional videos on improving sexual technique. None of these things will help him as long as he has shame and fear about being sexual or being a sexual being. Getting good sex is dependent on recovering Nice Guys bringing their shame and fear out of the closet and into the open where they can be looked at and released. *This step cannot be skipped!*

Most Nice Guys initially deny having any shame and fear about sex. Take the following quiz to see if you are in denial about your own sexual shame and fear.

1. Think back to your first sexual experience. Was it:

     a. A joyous experience which you could share with family and friends?

     b. Hidden, rushed, guilt-ridden, or in a less than ideal situation?

     c. Painful, abusive, or frightening?

2. When it comes to masturbation:

     a. Do you and your partner talk openly and comfortably about the subject?

     b. Would there be a crisis if your partner "caught" you doing it?

     c. Do you do it compulsively or in secret?

3. When it comes to your sexual experiences, thoughts, or impulses:

     a. You are comfortable revealing everything about yourself to your partner.

     b. You have secrets that you have never shared with anyone.

     c. Some aspect of your sexuality has caused a crisis in an intimate relationship.

     d. At some time in your life you have tried to eliminate or limit some problematic sexual behavior.

If you answered anything but "a" on any of the questions, you have sexual shame and fear. Read on.

---

Cleaning out sexual shame requires accepting, nonjudgmental people. A Nice Guy cannot do this work on his own. To release sexual shame and fear, the recovering Nice Guy must expose every aspect of his sexual self to safe, supportive people. This revealing allows the Nice Guy to release his shame and fear and free up the emotional energy it took to keep them hidden and repressed. These safe people can also give the Nice Guy supportive messages that it is not bad for him to be a sexual being.

Lyle, introduced earlier in the chapter, is a good example of how recovering Nice Guys can bring their sexual shame and fear out of the closet. Lyle was a good Christian, husband, and father who struggled with compulsive sexual behavior. Everything came crashing down for

Lyle when his wife found a phone bill and called some of the strange numbers. She was bewildered and devastated. Never in her wildest dreams (or nightmares) did she think that Lyle might be involved in anything like porography or phone sex. Little did she know she had just discovered the tip of the iceberg. Confronted with the evidence, Lyle initially feigned surprise and denied any knowledge of its origin. Finally, he broke down and told all. Well, almost all. It took several more weeks, several more emotional confrontations, and a call to me before everything came out.

After a couple of sessions of individual therapy, I suggested that Lyle start attending a 12-step group for sexual addicts. This idea initially terrified Lyle, but he knew he would have to do something radically different if he wanted to free himself of his compulsion and experience true sexual intimacy. To his surprise, revealing his long-kept secrets in the presence of other recovering sex addicts wasn't as difficult as he feared. In time, he began to look forward to the opportunity to talk about himself with safe people. Every time he revealed some secret thought or act, he felt a sense of relief, as if a weight had been lifted from his shoulders.

As Lyle revealed his fear and shame to safe people, he found that he was less interested in his hidden, compulsive behaviors. As he and his wife became more open and intimate with each other, he also began to enjoy a physical closeness with her that he had once tried to avoid. When Lyle came out of the closet, he began to heal a lifetime of hidden sexual behavior.

In my No More Mr. Nice Guy groups, I encourage recovering Nice Guys to bring their sexual shame out of the closet. I support them in talking explicitly about their sexuality. In our culture, most sex talk is done in pornographic, demeaning, moralizing, shaming, clinical, or joking ways. I invite recovering Nice Guys to reveal the ways they act out. I have them talk about their sexual history and early sexual experiences. I ask them to bring samples of pornography they find arousing. This is another way of releasing shame while also gaining important information.

Throughout the entire process of revealing themselves, I encourage recovering Nice Guys to experience whatever they may be feeling—shame, guilt, fear, arousal. At the same time, I give them supportive messages that what they are feeling is OK. There are so many negative messages in our society about male sexuality, it is difficult for Nice Guys to overcome their conditioning without this kind of encouragement and support.

---

Find a safe place to talk about the following issues:

*Your sexual history.* Discuss your earliest sexual memory, your childhood experiences, any sexual violation and trauma, any sexual issues in your family, your first sexual experience, your adult sexual history.

*Ways in which you have acted out sexually.* Discuss any way you may have acted out through affairs, prostitution, peep shows, 900 numbers, use of pornography, exhibitionism, fetishes, etc.

*Your dark side.* Discuss those things that even you have a hard time looking at in yourself-fantasies, rage, offending behavior.

---

## Taking Matters Into Their Own Hands Helps Nice Guys Get The Sex They Want

I regularly tell Nice Guys, "No one was put into this world to meet your needs but you." This is especially true with sex. When recovering Nice Guys decide to take responsibility for their own needs and take matters into their own hands, they put themselves in a position to get the quantity and quality of sex they want. Let me explain.

All significant behavior patterns are the sum of many, much smaller behavior patterns. The most effective way to change a behavior is to change its smallest elements. For example, if a Nice Guy is not getting as much sex as he wants or isn't getting the kind of sex he wants, the only way to change this behavior pattern is to change its smallest components. Rather than going out and trying to have more sex, it is more effective to change the little things that create the overall pattern of not getting much sex. Change the little things, and the big picture changes as a result.

Before Nice Guys can have exciting, passionate, and fulfilling sexual experiences with other people, they must learn how to have the same with themselves. By taking matters into their own hands—by practicing healthy masturbation—recovering Nice Guys can change the most basic dynamics that shape the bigger picture of how they do sex.

Consider the logic:

- Until a Nice Guy can be sexual with himself without shame, he won't be able to be sexual with another person without shame.

- Until a Nice Guy is comfortable giving pleasure to himself, he won't be able to receive pleasure from someone else.

- Until a Nice Guy can take responsibility for his own arousal and pleasure when he is by himself, he won't be able to take responsibility for his own arousal and pleasure when he is with someone else.

- Until a Nice Guy can be sexual with himself without using pornography or fantasy to distract himself, he won't be able to have sex with someone else without needing similar things to distract him.

Nice Guys can begin to change these dynamics by practicing what I call healthy masturbation. Healthy masturbation is a process of letting sexual energy unfold. It has no goal or destination. It's not just about orgasms. It does not require outside stimulation from pornography and doesn't use trances or fantasy to stay distracted from shame and fear. It is about learning to pay attention to what feels good. Most of all, it is about accepting sole responsibility for one's sexual pleasure and expression.

Many Nice Guys are initially uncomfortable with the discussion of healthy masturbation. The concept seems like an oxymoron. In general, Nice Guys have tremendous internalized shame around masturbation. They also frequently surround themselves with people who reinforce this shame (partner, religion, etc.). Many Nice Guys also struggle with compulsive masturbation. They fear that attempting any kind of self-gratification might open up Pandora's Box.

I have found that when recovering Nice Guys work on learning how to pleasure themselves without using fantasy or pornography, there is no way for their behavior to become compulsive. I have also found that when they share the experience with other nonjudgmental men, their shame diminishes rapidly.

---

## A NOTE ABOUT PORNOGRAPHY

I am not opposed to pornography legally or morally, but I think it is bad for men for several reasons:

- Pornography creates unrealistic expectations of what people should like and what sex should be like.

- Pornography addicts men to bodies and body parts.

- Pornography can easily become a substitute for a real sexual relationship.

- Pornography creates a trance in which men can be sexual while staying distracted from their shame and fear.

- Pornography compounds shame because it is usually hidden and used in secret.

I tell Nice Guys, if you are going to use pornography, do it openly. Doing so tends to break the trance and takes the buzz out of it.

---

## A NOTE ABOUT FANTASY

Fantasy is a form of dissociation—the process of separating one's body from one's mind. When a person fantasizes while being sexual he is purposefully and actively leaving his body. While some sex therapists advocate fantasy as a way of improving a sex life, it is actually the best way I know to kill it. Fantasizing during sex makes about as much sense as thinking about a Big Mac while eating a gourmet meal. About the only thing fantasy accomplishes is to distract a person from his shame and fear or cover up the fact that he is having bad sex.

Healthy masturbation helps the recovering Nice Guy change the core dynamics that prevent him from getting good sex. Healthy masturbation:

- Helps remove the shame and fear of being sexual
- Puts the Nice Guy in charge of his own sexual needs
- Removes dependency on unavailable partners or pornography
- Helps the Nice Guy learn to please the person that matters most—himself
- Gives the Nice Guy permission to have as much good sex as he wants
- Puts the Nice Guy in charge of his own pleasure

Changing these dynamics through healthy masturbation enhances and intensifies the experience of making love with another person. Terrance provides a good example.

Terrance originally came to therapy looking for a quick fix to his "problem" so his fiancée would not break up with him. In the first several sessions, I focused on the subject of him making his needs a priority. As with most Nice Guys, this initially made him uncomfortable (to put it mildly). Terrance was terrified that if he wasn't a great lover and didn't keep his girlfriend happy, she would leave him like his ex-wife did.

I began by encouraging Terrance to do a few nonsexual things just for himself. I reassured him regularly that this would make him more attractive to his fiancée, not less. As he began to discover that making his needs a priority didn't drive his girlfriend away, we took it to the next step. I talked with Terrance about healthy masturbation. I encouraged him to find a time when he would be undisturbed in which he could focus on his own pleasure and arousal. I suggested that he do this without having a goal of climaxing and without using fantasy or pornography. I encouraged him to pay attention to what felt good to him, and to observe the ways he unconsciously tried to distract himself from his shame and fear.

It took a few weeks for Terrance to carry out the assignment. The first time he tried it he reported not feeling "much of anything." I encouraged him to continue the assignment at least once a week. After a few weeks, he reported that he was actually beginning to enjoy pleasuring himself but felt some shame and fear that his fiancée would be mad at him.

I invited Terrance to bring his fiancée to therapy to work on shifting their sexual patterns. We talked about Terrance taking his focus off her arousal and orgasms and beginning to focus more on himself. His girlfriend actually expressed relief. She revealed that it felt like a burden when Terrance expected her to have multiple orgasms. Instead of telling him this in the past, she had just faked it.

As they communicated about their experience of making love, the patterns began to shift. They actually began spending more time talking with each other about what they liked and didn't like while they were having sex. Even though it was initially difficult, Terrance shared with his fiancée what he had found out about himself from his own healthy masturbation. He was surprised when she expressed interest in pleasuring him and having a reciprocal sexual relationship with him.

After a few months, Terrance and his fiancée got married as

planned. Both expressed how relieved they were to discard their old way of doing sex for a more intimate, connecting way.

---

Set aside a time to practice healthy masturbation. Choose a comfortable place where you will be undisturbed. Practice by looking at yourself and touching yourself without using pornography or fantasy. Pay attention to how it feels to experience your sexuality without any goals or agendas (such as having an orgasm). Also observe any tendency to distract yourself from what you are experiencing (going into fantasy, becoming goal-oriented, having distracting thoughts, loss of physical sensation). Just observe these experiences and use them as information about your shame and fear.

---

## Saying "No" To Bad Sex Helps Nice Guys Get The Sex They Want

When it comes to sex, Nice Guys are consummate bottom feeders. They settle for scraps and come back begging for more. Nice Guys settle for distorted images of bodies in pornography. They settle for the faceless sex of 900 numbers and chat rooms. They settle for trying to persuade unavailable people to begrudgingly be sexual with them. They settle for quick, compulsive masturbation. They settle for passionless, mechanical lovemaking. They settle for trances and fantasy. Nice Guys do a lot of settling.

As long as a Nice Guy is willing to settle for bad sex, he limits his opportunities to experience good sex. I regularly tell Nice Guys, "You have to be willing to let go of what you've got to get what you want." Good sex can occur only when a recovering Nice Guy decides to stop settling for bad sex!

So what does good sex look like? If we base our answer on what we see in movies or pornography, we will only keep perpetuating a formula for bad sex. Here is how I define "good sex."

Good sex consists of two people taking full responsibility for meeting their own needs. It has no goal. It is free of agendas and expectations. Rather than being a performance, it is an unfolding of sexual energy. It is about two people revealing themselves in the most intimate and vulnerable of ways. Good sex occurs when two people focus on their own pleasure, passion, and arousal, and stay connected to those same things in their partner. All of these dynamics allow good sex to unfold in unpredictable, spontaneous, and memorable ways.

When recovering Nice Guys decide they will no longer settle for anything less than good sex, they begin to take responsibility for doing something different.

- They let go of the concept of being a great lover
- They practice being clear and direct
- They choose available partners
- They don't settle for scraps
- They decide that bad sex is not better than no sex

Aaron is a good example of what can happen when a recovering Nice Guy decides to say "no" to bad sex. For the first few weeks in the No More Mr. Nice Guy group, Aaron vented his frustrations and shared how helpless he felt to get Hannah to want to have sex with him. It was obvious that Aaron believed his wife held the key to his sexual happiness and that he was angry over her willful refusal to use that key. As a result, he felt rejected and worthless.

After a few weeks, I suggested that Aaron go on a sexual moratorium in which he refrained from having sex with Hannah for a period of six months. During this time, I suggested that he focus on doing things he had given up when he and Hannah got married. I also encouraged him to tell Hannah whatever he was feeling. I shared with him that a sexual moratorium would make it easier for him to do these things because he wouldn't be so concerned about maintaining the possibility of her availability. If they weren't having sex, he wouldn't have to worry about doing something that might make her angry and cause her to withhold sex.

At first, Aaron was bewildered as to how this plan could get Hannah to want to have more sex with him. I told him the goal was not to get her to have more sex, but for him to reclaim his key and stop feeling like a victim.

Even though he was initially hesitant, he acknowledged that he wasn't having much sex anyway. With the support of the men in the group, Aaron decided to go home that night and tell his wife what he planned to do.

The next week, Aaron shared with the group what he had told his wife. He reported that she was initially angry, but over the course of the week had acted more loving toward him than she had in months.

Over the next six months, Aaron shared his experiences with the group. On several occasions he reported doing things for himself that previously would have created tremendous anxiety. He went out with some guy friends he hadn't seen in a couple of years. He began to share his feelings with his wife. On more than one occasion, this included telling her when he was angry at her. He even let her know on a couple of occasions when he wasn't in the mood to listen to her talk about her problems. He also found that he became more honest—revealing things to her that he had previously kept to himself.

Aaron also reported that his wife had made some sexual advances toward him. She revealed to him that since he was not pursuing her, she felt freer to move toward him. She also expressed that she liked being able to have sexual energy with Aaron, without it always having to end up in intercourse.

After six months, Aaron reported feeling less resentful and much closer to his wife. He also discovered how to get his needs met and express his feelings more directly, instead of through sex. Most importantly, when he and Hannah did start having sex again, he felt much more connected to his wife.

---

**BREAKING FREE:**
# ACTIVITY
## 39

Consider going on a sexual moratorium. Consciously refrain from sex for a predetermined period of time. No matter what your sexual situation is, it can be a powerful learning experience. Most guys initially resist the idea, but once they make the decision to do it, they find it to be a very positive experience. A sexual moratorium can have many benefits:

- Helps break dysfunction cycles
- Eliminates pursuing and distancing
- Releases resentment
- Allows the Nice Guy to see that he can live without sex
- Helps the Nice Guy realize that no one else but him holds the key to his sexual experience
- Helps the Nice Guy see how he settles for bad sex
- Eliminates fear that the Nice Guy's partner can withhold sex or approval
- Helps the Nice Guy pay attention to the meaning of sexual impulses: whenever the Nice Guy feels the impulse to be sexual, he can automatically ask himself, "Why am I feeling sexual?"
- Helps break addictive patterns by eliminating compulsive masturbation, pornography, and other addictive behaviors
- Helps the Nice Guy begin to address feelings he has been avoiding with sex

Before beginning a sexual moratorium, discuss it with your partner. It helps to set a specific time. I suggest three to six months. It can be done.

Decide on the parameters of the moratorium. Once you have begun, pay attention to slips and sabotaging behaviors, from both you and your partner. Remember, it is a learning experience. You don't have to do it perfectly.

---

## Following The Example Of The Bull Moose Helps Nice Guys Get The Sex They Want

In nature, the alpha male and the bull moose don't sit around trying to figure out what will make the girls like them. They are just themselves: fierce, strong, competitive, and sexually proud. Because they are what they are and do what they do, prospective mates are attracted.

As in nature, the greatest aphrodisiac is self-confidence. As recovering Nice Guys become comfortable just being themselves, they begin to look more attractive. Self-respect, courage, and integrity look good on a man. As recovering Nice Guys chart their own path and put themselves first, people respond.

I've listened to recovering Nice Guys tell of "selfishly" putting their needs first and then being surprised when a seemingly unavailable partner expresses a desire to be sexual. One client, who hadn't had sex with his wife in 14 months, shared in a Nice Guy group that he was tired of listening to his wife complain about her work problems. That night, for the first time in 15 years of marriage, he told his wife that he was too tired to listen. Even though she was initially angry, later that night she asked him if he wanted to make love.

## A Force Of Nature

The very thing that makes sex so exciting is exactly what makes it so terifying. Sex is powerful, chaotic, and wild. It crackles with cosmic energy. It draws us like a moth to a flame. As recovering Nice Guys release their sexual shame and fear, take responsibility for their own pleasure, refuse to settle for bad sex, and practice being just who they are, they put themselves in the position to embrace this cosmic force without fear or reservation. This is when the sex really gets good.

chapter **NINE**

# GET THE LIFE YOU WANT: DISCOVER YOUR PASSION AND PURPOSE IN LIFE, WORK, AND CAREER

If there were no limits on your life:

- Where would you live?
- What would you be doing in your leisure time?
- What kind of work would you be engaged in?
- What would your home and surroundings look like?

As you look at the reality of your life, ask yourself two questions: First, are you creating the life you want? Second, if not, why not?

In general, the Nice Guys with whom I have worked have been intelligent, industrious, and competent individuals. While most are at least moderately successful, the majority have not lived up to their full abilities or potential. Nor have they created the kind of life they really desire.

Since Nice Guys spend so much time seeking approval, hiding

their flaws, playing it safe, and doing the opposite of what works, it makes sense that they would typically fall short of being all they can be. This is perhaps the greatest tragedy wrought by the Nice Guy Syndrome—countless intelligent and talented men wasting their lives and wallowing in the mire of mediocrity.

## Nice Guys On The Job

Most Nice Guys initially come to counseling to deal with the way their life paradigm is affecting their intimate relationships. These relationship problems often overshadow the reality that they are equally dissatisfied with their job, career, or life direction in general. The dynamics that keep Nice Guys stuck in dysfunctional, unsatisfying relationships are often the same dynamics that keep them stuck in dysfunctional and unsatisfying vocations.

There are numerous reasons why Nice Guys tend to be less than they can be in life, work, and career. These include:

- Fear
- Trying to do it right
- Trying to do everything themselves
- Self-sabotage
- A distorted self-image
- Deprivation thinking
- Staying stuck in familiar but dysfunctional systems

## Fear Prevents Nice Guys From Getting The Life They Want

If I were to identify one common factor at the core of every problem experienced by Nice Guys, it would be *fear*. Pretty much everything Nice Guys do or don't do is governed by fear. Their thoughts are funneled through fear-encrusted neurons in their brains. Their interactions are dictated by the politics of fear.

- It is fear that prevents a Nice Guy from demanding the raise he has been promised.
- It is fear that keeps a Nice Guy from going back to school to get the education or training he needs to pursue a truly fulfilling career.
- It is fear that prevents a Nice Guy from quitting a job he despises.
- It is fear that gets in the way of a Nice Guy starting the business of his dreams.
- It is fear that prevents a Nice Guy from living where he really wants to live and doing what he really wants to do.

Nice Guys are afraid of making a mistake, afraid of doing it wrong, afraid of failure, afraid of losing it all. Right alongside these fears of disaster is the paradoxical *fear of success*. Nice Guys are typically afraid that if they are truly successful:

- They will be found out to be frauds
- They won't be able to live up to people's expectations
- They will be criticized
- They won't be able to handle the increased expectations
- They will lose control over their lives
- They will do something to mess up everything

Rather than facing these fears—real or imagined—Nice Guys typically settle for operating at a fraction of their full potential.

## Trying To Do It Right Prevents Nice Guys From Getting the Life They Want

The essence of all life is evolution and change. In order for this process to occur naturally and completely in an individual, a person has to be willing to let go of control. Letting go allows the beautiful, serendipitous chaos of creation to resonate through one's self. The result is a dynamic, fulfilling life.

Nice Guys are obsessed with trying to keep their lives smooth and uneventful. They do this by trying to "do it right" and following the "rules." Unfortunately, this life strategy is the most effective way to put a lid on any creative life energy. This lid kills their passion and prevents Nice Guys from living up to their full potential.

- Trying to do it right robs Nice Guys of their creativity and productivity.
- Striving for perfection keeps Nice Guys focused on their imperfections.
- Seeking external validation and approval keeps Nice Guys stuck in mediocrity.
- Attempting to hide flaws and mistakes prevents Nice Guys from taking risks or trying something new.
- Following the rules make Nice Guys rigid, cautious, and fearful.

It is because of these self-imposed limits that many Nice Guys are dissatisfied, bored, or unhappy with their life and vocation.

## Trying To Do Everything Themselves Prevents Nice Guys From Getting The Life They Want

As children, Nice Guys did not get their needs met in timely, judicious ways. Some were neglected, some were used, some were abused, some were abandoned. All grew up believing that it was a bad or dangerous thing for them to have needs. All grew up convinced that if they were going to have anything in life, it would be up to them.

Consequently, Nice Guys are terrible receivers. They are terrified of asking for help. They are completely miserable when others try to give to them. They have difficulty delegating to others.

Because they believe they have to do it all themselves, Nice Guys rarely live up to their full potential. Nobody can be good at everything or succeed all on their own. Nice Guys believe they should be able to. They might be jacks-of-all-trades, but they are typically masters of none. This childhood conditioning ensures that they will never be all they can be in any area of life.

## Self-Sabotage Prevents Nice Guys From Getting The Life They Want

Because of their fear of success, Nice Guys are masters of self-sabotage. They undermine their success by:

- Wasting time
- Making excuses
- Not finishing projects
- Caretaking other people
- Having too many projects going at once
- Getting caught up in chaotic relationships
- Procrastinating
- Not setting boundaries

Nice Guys are typically good at appearing competent. But to be really great—to really rise to the top—invites too much unwanted attention and scrutiny. The bright lights of success threaten to illuminate their self-perceived cracks and flaws.

Consequently, Nice Guys find many creative ways to make sure they are never too successful. If they don't start something, they won't fail. If they don't finish something, they won't be criticized. If they have too much going on at once, they won't have to do any one thing well. If they have enough good excuses, people won't expect too much of them.

# A Distorted Self-Image Prevents
# Nice Guys From Getting the Life They Want

Because their needs were not met in a timely, judicious fashion in childhood, Nice Guys developed a distorted view of themselves. With a naive, immature logic they came to the conclusion that if their needs were not important, neither were they. This is the basis of their toxic shame. At their core, all Nice Guys believe they are not important or good enough.

If a Nice Guy was called on to take care of a critical, needy, or dependent parent, he received a double dose of toxic shame. A child believes he should be able to please a critical parent, fix the problems of a depressed parent, and meet the needs of a smothering parent. Unfortunately, he can't.

*As a result of their inability to fix, please, or take care of one or more parents, many Nice Guys developed a deep-seated sense of inadequacy.* They believed they should be able to do the job. Nevertheless, they never could seem to do it right or good enough—mom was still depressed, dad was still critical.

This internalized sense of inadequacy and defectiveness is carried into adulthood. Some Nice Guys compensate by trying to do everything right. They hope that by doing so, no one will ever find out how inadequate they are. Other Nice Guys just give up before they try.

This feeling of inadequacy prevents Nice Guys from making themselves visible, taking chances, or trying something new. It keeps them in the same old rut, never seeing how talented and intelligent they really are. Everyone around them can see these things, but their distorted childhood lenses won't let them accurately see their true potential and ability.

The result of this distorted self-image is an *emotional and cognitive glass ceiling*. This invisible lid prevents Nice Guys from being all they can be. If they do try to rise above it, they bump their heads and tumble down to more familiar territory.

## Deprivation Thinking Prevents
## Nice Guys From Getting The Life They Want

Not having their needs adequately met in childhood created a belief for Nice Guys that there wasn't enough of what they needed to go around. This deprivation experience became the lens through which they viewed the world.

This paradigm of scarcity and deprivation makes Nice Guys manipulative and controlling. It causes them to believe they better hang on to what they've got and not take too many chances. It leads them to resent other people who seem to have what they lack.

Because of their deprivation thinking, Nice Guys think small. They don't believe they deserve to have good things. They find all kinds of ways to make sure their view of the world is never challenged. They settle for scraps and think it is all they deserve. They create all kinds of rationalizations to explain why they will never have what they really desire. Because of their self-fulfilling beliefs, Nice Guys rarely live up to their potential or get what they really want in life.

## Staying Stuck In Dysfunctional,
## But Familiar Systems Prevents Nice Guys From
## Getting The Life They Want

As stated in previous chapters, two major factors prevent Nice Guys from getting what they want in love. The first is that they tend to re-create familiar yet dissatisfying relationships. They find partners who will help them create the same dysfunctional kinds of relationships they experienced as children. These men then frequently see themselves as being victims to the dysfunction of their partners. Nice Guys have a difficult time seeing that they were attracted to these people for a reason.

Second, Nice Guys rarely experience the kind of relationships they want because they are bad enders. When a healthy person would pack up and move on, Nice Guys just keep doing more of the same, hoping that something will miraculously change.

Nice Guys aren't much different in their jobs. They are attracted to careers and work situations that allow them to re-create the dysfunctional roles, relationships, and rules of their childhood. They often see themselves as helpless victims to these situations. Rarely do they see why they need these systems to be the way they are, and that they have the choice to leave.

Unconsciously re-creating familiar family patterns in their jobs and careers keeps Nice Guys stuck and dissatisfied. While they are perpetuating the dysfunction of their childhood, they rarely do what they really want or rise to the top of their chosen vocation.

## Realizing Your Passion And Potential

I frequently tell the men in my No More Mr. Nice Guy groups that my goal is for every one of them to leave the group a millionaire. This statement really has very little to do with money or material wealth—it is about discovering passion and living up to potential.

As stated above, the Nice Guys I counsel are generally intelligent, talented men. As these men work on recovering from the Nice Guy Syndrome, they begin to accept themselves just as they are. This acceptance of the self allows them to embrace their passions and face their fears.

The formation of a more accurate view of the self and the world allows the abundance of the universe to begin flowing freely into their lives. Sometimes this takes the form of money. Sometimes it takes the form of love. Sometimes it takes the form of sex. Sometimes it takes the form of the bright lights of fame. Sometimes it includes all of the above.

The remainder of this chapter presents a strategy to help recovering Nice Guys become all they can be. The following pages present a plan that has already helped countless Nice Guys discover their passion and live up to their potential. It can do the same for you.

## Facing Fears Allows Nice Guys
## To Get The Life They Want

Charlie could have been the poster child for passionless, underachieving Nice Guys. When I first met Charlie, he was stuck in a job he hated and living a life characterized by mediocrity and fear. Charlie had completed his engineering degree a couple of years before, yet he was still working at the same job he had held before starting college. Charlie's employers had promised him a big promotion upon graduation. When they failed to keep their promise, Charlie just stifled his resentment and kept on doing the same old thing he had always done.

Charlie's single passion was flying. In spite of warnings of disaster from his mother, he had begun taking flying lessons after he finished college. Though Charlie dreamed of earning his pilot's license, he never seemed to be able to complete the necessary requirements to achieve his goal.

A woman at his work introduced Charlie to my website. When he read the description of a Nice Guy he was mortified. He couldn't figure out how someone could know him so well. It took him six months before he worked up the nerve to send me an e-mail. It took him another two months to send me a second. From the first time Charlie looked at my website he knew he needed to join a men's group, but the idea of being that vulnerable terrified him.

It was at that point that Charlie made a decision that changed his life. Charlie decided that if something frightened him that much, he needed to face his fear and do it. Little did he know then, but that decision was just the beginning of a journey that would lead Charlie toward the rediscovery of his passion and purpose in life.

Over the next year and a half Charlie lived by one credo: If he was afraid of something, he confronted that fear. Charlie's progress was slow but steady. Basically, he crawled until he could walk. He took baby steps until he could run. Once he got going, there was no stopping him.

Over a period of about eighteen months, Charlie took several steps toward rediscovering his passion and purpose in life.

He became more and more active in his No More Mr. Nice Guy men's group, revealing himself and confronting fellow group members.

He began looking at the neglect he experienced and the distorted fear-based messages he received in his family.

He asked his father to come to counseling with him where he confronted him on his unavailability and lack of concern for his well being in childhood.

He quit blaming his lack of money for flying lessons on his girlfriend.

He changed flying schools when his current school was unable to provide him with the type of instruction and equipment he needed.

He began interviewing for jobs that took advantage of his engineering degree.

He began confronting his feelings of inadequacy, family messages about playing it safe, and distorted beliefs about his qualifications as an engineer.

He confronted his girlfriend (whom he was initially terrified of) about her lack of participation in household responsibilities.

He took his solo flight and got his pilot's license.

He allowed his men's group to take him out for his birthday to a restaurant where he faced his fear of being the center of attention.

He applied for and got a job with an engineering firm that expressed a belief that he was capable, talented, and had something to offer their company.

When Charlie told the group about getting the job, I realized that I had witnessed a metamorphosis of epic proportions. Charlie had gone from being an introverted, frightened, and passive Nice Guy, to an evolving man with passion and purpose.

I asked Charlie to send me an e-mail with his formula for success. Here is what he wrote:

*Bob,*
*Here is roughly how I arrived at the new job:*

1. *Very first, before anything else could happen, I had to stop being a victim.*
2. *I began by setting boundaries. At first they were small ones and they grew with time.*
3. *From the boundaries being set and respected, I started believing in myself.*
4. *Honesty came along somewhere during this time.*
5. *Believing that I am an adult, I have an education, and I am qualified to take on the role of an industrial engineer.*
6. *I always knew that my previous employer was dysfunctional, and that it was comfortable for a reason. When I finally realized and accepted that I did not need that system to survive, I could finally move on.*

*Charlie*

## Charting Their Own Path Allows Nice Guys To Get The Life They Want

Most folks—Nice Guys included—do not consciously take responsibility for creating the kind of life they want. Most people just accept where they are, and act as if they have little power in shaping an exciting, productive, and fulfilling life.

When I talk with Nice Guys about taking charge of their lives, most have a difficult time wrapping their brain around the concept. It just doesn't fit their paradigm that they can make choices and act to make these choices a reality.

I encourage Nice Guys to visualize creating a life where they do what they love and get paid for it. Most of them have difficulty with this concept. They act as if I am asking them to believe a fairy tale. Occasionally they will dismiss the idea with the excuse, "Not everybody can be lucky like you (referring to me) and have a job they really love and get paid well for it, too." For a while, I accepted this logic until it dawned on me that the life I was living had nothing to do with luck.

Earning a Ph.D. involved a conscious decision, persistence, and hard work—not luck.

Building a counseling practice involved facing fears, quitting a secure, well-paying job, making sacrifices, working a second job to pay bills, learning by trial and error, and a living through a period of poverty—not luck.

Developing my skills as a therapist involved a commitment to personal growth, constant evolution, and a financial investment in my own therapeutic process—not luck.

Writing a book, building a website, and getting published required persistence and the confrontation of numerous fears—not luck.

I'm not anything special. I'm an ordinary guy with ordinary talents. I have many of the same fears as the Nice Guys with whom I work. I don't have any special talent or skill that the majority of my clients don't have.

What's the difference?

- A conscious decision to face fears
- A conscious decision to not settle for mediocrity
- A conscious decision to make my own rules

Think about the people you respect or look up to. Most probably started with nothing but still found ways to create interesting, productive, and passionate lives. These people charted their own paths and made their own rules. What makes them different? Most are just ordinary people who took charge of their lives.

Here's the good news—if they can do it, so can you. One of my favorite affirmations is, *What one man can do, another man can do.* Think about it—if others have taken charge and created lives worth emulating, so can you. *The only thing stopping you from having the kind of life you really want is you.* It is time to start charting your own path, making your own rules, and making your dreams a reality.

---

**BREAKING FREE:**
# ACTIVITY
## 40

Look over the list below. Choose one of the items and name a tangible fear from your life. Write down how you will confront that specific issue. Then, take a small step toward facing that fear. Ask someone to encourage and support you. Don't try to do it alone.

Remember, no matter what happens, you will handle it.

- Ask for a raise or promotion
- Quit an unsatisfying job
- Start your own business
- Go back to school
- Confront a conflict situation
- Promote an idea or something you have created
- Pursue a lifelong goal
- Spend more time with a hobby or interest

---

## Letting Go Of Trying To Do It Right Allows Nice Guys To Get The Life They Want

This book began as a few chapters I planned to write to give to the men in my first No More Mr. Nice Guy group. Initially, when there was no agenda or goal, my writing was a spontaneous recording of my growing insight into the Nice Guy Syndrome. Before long, clients and family members began suggesting that I write a book. It seemed like a logical extension of what I was already doing, so the idea made perfect sense.

It was at that time that something began to change. Rather than being just a few insights and illustrations written for the benefit of a handful of clients, my effort became directed at producing something that would be deserving of publication and widespread distribution. I began hearing people suggest things like "best-seller," *Oprah,* and "get rich."

What was once an effortless labor of love began to falter under the weight of expectation. In order to live up to the lofty standards people were suggesting, my book had better be good. Not just good—perfect!

With that agenda I labored for six years to complete *No More Mr. Nice Guy.* The most common question I was asked by friends and family during this time was, "When are you going to finish your book?"

Over the years the manuscript went through at least three major revisions as well as extensive editing. Numerous factors contributed to the length of time it took to finish the book, but the number one reason was that I thought it had to be perfect. I thought the book had to be perfect to be published. I thought it had to be perfect for anyone to buy it. I thought it had to be perfect for it to help anyone.

Unfortunately, this gross misperception had a number of detrimental consequences: I believed I had to write everything I knew about the Nice Guy Syndrome. (The original manuscript of this book was probably four times its present length.) I believed I had to be an eloquent writer. I believed the text had to be flawless.

I went to therapy to find out why I couldn't finish my book. My children became disillusioned, predicting that I never would finish. My wife half-seriously threatened to leave me if I didn't finish.

Finally, after years of frustration, I had a breakthrough. A very wise person suggested that I give myself permission to never publish the book. I felt an immediate sense of relief.

I realized that I had gotten away from my original goal—to write a few insights that would help a few men live better lives. Once I let go of the burden of having to get published, be a best-selling author, and appear on *Oprah,* everything changed. I went back to my original agenda. From then on when I wrote, I only asked myself one thing: "Will this help my clients find answers to their problems?" I also kept reminding myself that my clients would never get a chance to benefit from my insight if I never finished the book.

Once I gave up the belief that *No More Mr. Nice Guy* had to be perfect, things began to fall into place. I completed the book. Clients reported that it was changing their lives. Therapists began to request copies for their clients. Radio talk show hosts and newspaper and magazine writers began contacting me for interviews. I hired an agent. Publishers began pursuing me.

*Trying to do it right* only sucked the life out of *No More Mr. Nice Guy.* Letting go and letting it just be "good enough" set me free to embrace my passion and create something of lasting value. This same principle applies to every area of the recovering Nice Guy's life.

---

### BREAKING FREE:
# ACTIVITY
## 41

What do you really want in life? What prevents you from making it happen? Write down three things you want to make happen in your life. Then write a personal affirmation that will take you where you want to go and post it on a sheet of paper where you can see it. Share your dreams and your affirmation with a safe person.

---

### BREAKING FREE:
# ACTIVITY
## 42

How does your perfectionism or need to do it right get in the way of realizing your passion and potential? Pick one thing that you have always wanted to do: write a book, turn your hobby into a business, move, go back to school, fully embrace a talent.

Now, ask yourself the question: if you knew ahead of time that this endeavor would be a success, would you hesitate to do it? Would this knowledge set you free from the belief that you have to do it perfectly? Would this knowledge motivate you to get started or complete what you have already begun? What risks would you be willing to take if you knew ahead of time that there was no way for you to fail?

What are you waiting for? Let go of the need to do it perfectly and just do it!

---

## Learning To Ask For Help Allows Nice Guys To Get The Life They Want

A major reason Nice Guys frequently fail to live up to their potential is that they believe they have to do everything themselves. Phil is a good example.

Phil's goal in life was to be rich. He seemed to have a lot of things going for him: He was good looking, intelligent, outgoing, and funny. Yet Phil always seemed to fall way short of achieving his lofty goals and dreams. A number of things got in the way—taking short-cuts, procrastination, and insecurities about whether he deserved to get what he really wanted.

Perhaps Phil's greatest roadblock was his difficulty asking people for help. Phil had a number of faulty core beliefs about people helping him. He didn't believe he deserved to get what he wanted. He didn't believe his needs were important to other people. He believed the surest way not to get his needs met was to ask in clear and direct ways.

One day in his No More Mr. Nice Guy men's group, Phil was lamenting about the lack of sex in his relationship with his wife. I asked Phil if he asked his wife to have sex with him. He said "no." I asked him if he believed his wife wanted to have sex with him. To this he also replied in the negative.

I told Phil that I thought his lack of sex was symptomatic of a bigger problem in his life—him not thinking his needs were important and not believing that other people wanted to help him meet his needs. I suggested that changing his beliefs about his sexual needs might be the place to begin changing core beliefs that prevented him from having other things he wanted in life.

The next week, Phil was grinning from ear to ear. "My wife and I had sex," he beamed. The group shared in his enthusiasm. They wanted to know how it happened.

"I asked," was Phil's simple reply.

I questioned Phil how his wife felt about having sex with him. "She was fine about it," he replied. "She said she likes having sex with me, but that I hadn't asked in a long time so she didn't think I was interested."

A week later, Phil told the group he was dreading asking his father-in-law to borrow money to get the old single-pane windows replaced on his house. Some of the group members began asking questions about the cost. Some shared that they had done that kind of project before. I suggested that Phil ask the group to help him. It was like pulling teeth, but Phil asked the men if they would help him replace his windows. The members of the group responded unanimously that they would be glad to. About a month later, the men got together at Phil's house and had the equivalent of an old fashioned barn raising.

These two experiences had a tremendous impact on Phil. He began to see that his needs were important, that people wanted to help him meet his needs, and that the surest way of getting people to help was to ask.

Phil began to build on this new paradigm. Within a few weeks he shared a plan with the group to start his own business. A friend of the family had offered to help him get started in his own landscaping business. This prospect especially excited him because the seasonal work would allow him to teach snowboarding during the winter—a lifelong dream.

An old friend offered to be his financial backer. His wife volunteered to look for a job that paid health insurance benefits. Men in the group offered to help him write a business plan and set up his bookkeeping.

As long as Phil tried to do everything himself, he struggled to get what he wanted. Once he started asking for help and letting people be there for him, his life began to turn around. He is now headed in the direction of creating the kind of life and vocation he has always dreamed of.

## Identifying Self-Sabotaging Behaviors Allows Nice Guys To Get The Life They Want

As mentioned earlier in the chapter, Nice Guys find numerous creative ways to sabotage their success in life. They waste time, they procrastinate, they start things but don't finish, they spend too much time fixing other people's problems, they distract themselves with trivial pursuits, they create chaos, they make excuses.

Sal is a good example of this. Sal was raised by a passive father and a schizophrenic mother. Neither parent was available to pay attention to him or meet his needs. At a young age he had to take responsibility for the welfare of his younger brother. Sal had virtually no options as a child. When he felt frightened or overwhelmed, he would just hunker down and trudge ahead with dogged determination.

As an adult, Sal ran a body shop for his uncle. His uncle was a cheap, short-sighted, marginally involved business owner. It was Sal's job to create a profitable business with the limited resources and dissatisfied employees his uncle provided. (Sal actually operated on the assumption that this feat could be successfully accomplished!)

Every week when Sal came to men's group, his first order of business was to pop a couple of Tylenol to quiet the stress headache created by trying to negotiate an impossible situation at work. On one occasion, I asked Sal if he wanted to explore options for his work situation.

"What's the use?" he replied. "There's nothing that can be done."

For about fifteen minutes, group members asked questions and proposed options. Sal looked like a man undergoing a root canal with no anesthetic.

"Could you talk with your uncle and let him know how difficult your job is with the resources he gives you?"

"I've tried that. He doesn't care."

"Could you offer profit sharing to motivate your employees?"

"My uncle is too cheap. He would never go for it."

"Could you hire an assistant to help with the work load?"

"We tried that once and it didn't work out."

"Could you get out of management and go back to painting cars?"

"I would make more money, but it is too toxic."

"Could you get out of the auto body business and do something else?"

"Like what? I've got a mortgage, a wife, and two kids. How am I supposed to start over now?"

"What is your passion, your dream job?"

This time Sal paused for a moment before answering. "I've always wanted to teach martial arts. There is no way it could ever happen though. I'd have to work evenings and weekends. My wife just wouldn't go for that, and I'd be away from the kids too much."

With each question asked and each option proposed, Sal grew noticeably tenser. His eyes reflected a terror as if he was being interrogated by Gestapo agents with cattle prods and ice picks. When it became apparent that exploring possible options only aggravated his fear and caused him to shut down further, the group members mercifully backed off. Later, Sal referred to the experience as "being reamed by the group."

In most situations, Nice Guys aren't victims to others, they victimize themselves. By his attitudes and actions, Sal all but guaranteed that he would never experience any kind of success or satisfaction in his job. It was much more familiar and comfortable to stay stuck in a stressful, no-win situation.

Every Nice Guy with whom I have worked has at some point had to make a conscious decision to stop sabotaging himself. This is a crucial aspect in recovery from the Nice Guy Syndrome. In order to start getting what they want in life, work, and career, recovering Nice Guys have to make the conscious decision to get out of their own way.

One way of doing this is by changing the way they think about change. This begins with Nice Guys becoming aware of why they unconsciously create so many barriers that keep them feeling stuck. A mortgage, a wife, a lack of a degree, debt, children—are all just excuses. Making significant life changes doesn't require chucking all these things. It means seeing them for what they really are—excuses—and taking small steps in the direction one wants to be going.

For example, Sal could begin teaching martial arts one evening per week. He could begin working at paying down personal debt to enable him to change jobs in the future. He could refocus time spent on trivial, unsatisfying activities.

---

**BREAKING FREE:**
# ACTIVITY
## 43

Do you believe your needs are important? Do you believe other people want to help you meet your needs?

On a sheet of paper, make a list of helpers you have in your life right now. These can be friends and family members, they can be professionals, such as doctors, lawyers, therapists, and CPAs. After making the list, answer the following questions:

- What kind of helpers do you still need?
- How can you use these helpers more effectively?
- How do you prevent these people from helping you?

Start looking for opportunities to ask these people for help. Build networks. Before asking for help, repeat the affirmation: This person wants to help me get my needs met.

## BREAKING FREE:
# ACTIVITY
## 44

Identify how you sabotage yourself. Once you have identified your patterns, determine what you have to do differently to get what you really want. Review each item below and identify specific behaviors that will help you stop sabotaging yourself and achieve your goals.

- Focus
- Do it now
- Accept "good enough" rather than "perfect"
- Finish what you start
- Don't start new projects until the old ones are completely finished
- Don't make excuses
- Detach from other people's problems

Share your strategy with a safe person. Check in with them on a regular basis to monitor how you are doing (failing to do this part would be an effective way to sabotage yourself).

## BREAKING FREE:
# ACTIVITY
## 45

Set this book down for a few moments and close your eyes. Take a couple of deep breaths and exhale slowly. Clear your mind.

Once you are relaxed, picture yourself living in an abundant world. In this abundant world, there are no restraints or limitations. Good things flow past you continuously. Imagine every abundant thing you have ever desired—car, home, friends, love, joy, wealth, success, peace of mind, challenge. Visualize yourself living your life surrounded by this abundance.

Repeat this visualization several times a day until it begins to feel real to you. Open your arms, your heart, and your mind. Get out of the way, and let it happen.

## Developing A More Accurate View Of The World Allows Nice Guys To Get The Life They Want

Ever wonder why other people seem to have so much more than you—more money, a better job, a nice car, a prettier wife? Do you envy these people? Do you resent them for having what you don't? Do you wonder when it will be your turn?

Due to their early life experiences, Nice Guys tend to be ruled by deprivation thinking. They believe there is only so much to go around, and if someone else already has a lot there is less for them.

Nice Guys have a difficult time comprehending that we live in an abundant, ever-expanding universe. They tend to see the goodies as being in short supply. They hang on tightly to what they've got, fearing there won't be more when it is gone. They believe they have to control and manipulate to ensure that what little is out there won't go away. They play it safe, not trusting that their needs will always be abundantly met.

This paradigm of scarcity can be illustrated by a Nice Guy named Russell. As a successful salesman, Russell earned a comfortable six-figure income. He religiously put forty percent of his take home pay into savings and investments. He kept a minimum balance of $30,000 in his checking account. In spite of his ability to create financial wealth, Russell was controlled by his deprivation thinking. Russell was so afraid of financial ruin that he would not allow his wife to buy a $9.00 video for his children at Costco if it wasn't in the budget.

Russell's deprivation thinking in regard to money was a reflection of his view of the world in general. His father was miserly and rigid. He seemed to single Russell out for critical treatment, while heaping praise and favor on his two brothers. Later, before he died, his father cut Russell out of his will and gave Russell's share to the church. It is no wonder that Russell viewed the world through lenses clouded by deprivation.

When we come to see the world as a place of abundance, we

come to realize that there is plenty for everyone. Everything we need is flowing by us—all we have to do is get out of the way of our own small thinking and let it come.

---

# ACTIVITY
## 46

Read over the list of rules below. Try a few of them on for size. Add to the list your own personal rules. Write these rules on note cards and put them where you can see them every day.

- If it frightens you, do it.
- Don't settle. Every time you settle, you get exactly what you settled for.
- Put yourself first.
- No matter what happens, you will handle it.
- Whatever you do, do it one hundred percent.
- If you do what you have always done, you will get what you have always got.
- You are the only person on this planet responsible for your needs, wants, and happiness.
- Ask for what you want.
- If what you are doing isn't working, try something different.
- Be clear and direct.
- Learn to say "no."
- Don't make excuses.
- If you are an adult, you are old enough to make your own rules.
- Let people help you.
- Be honest with yourself.
- Do not let anyone treat you badly. No one. Ever.
- Remove yourself from a bad situation instead of waiting for the situation to change.
- Don't tolerate the intolerable—ever.
- Stop blaming. Victims never succeed.
- Live with integrity. Decide what feels right to you, then do it.
- Accept the consequences of your actions.
- Be good to yourself.

- Think "abundance."
- Face difficult situations and conflict head on.
- Don't do anything in secret.
- Do it now.
- Be willing to let go of what you have so you can get what you want.
- Have fun. If you are not having fun, something is wrong.
- Give yourself room to fail. There are no mistakes, only learning experiences.
- Control is an illusion. Let go. Let life happen.

---

Look around at the wealth—the cars people drive, the houses they live in, the trips they take. You can't argue with the sheer material abundance that can be created in our world. If other people are living full, abundant lives, why not you? Remember, *what one man can do, another man can do.*

- If one man can make a million dollars, why can't you?
- If one man can start the business of his dreams, why can't you?
- If one man can drive a Mercedes, why can't you?
- If one man can quit a crummy job and find a better one, why can't you?
- If one man can be a snowboarding instructor, why can't you?

Unfortunately, the world can't give us something that we're not ready to receive. Since deprivation thinking keeps a person holding tightly to what he already has, there is no receptivity for receiving more. As Phil found out, when we ask for what we want, and expect to receive it, it will come one way or another.

## Get The Life You Want: The No More Mr. Nice Guy Strategy For Success

Nice Guys believe there is a set of rules that govern all behavior. They are convinced that if they can figure out these rules and successfully abide by them, they will have a smooth, happy life. They also believe that there are dire consequences for failing to discern and obey these rules.

Discovering passion and purpose requires figuring out what works and what doesn't. Mature, successful people establish their own rules. These rules are measured by only one standard: *do they work?*

Over the years, the men in my No More Mr. Nice Guy groups have discovered a number of rules that work for them. These rules have helped them discover their passion and live up to their potential. These rules have helped them create the kind of life and vocation they really desire.

It is time to start getting what you want. Breaking free from the Nice Guy Syndrome will allow you to discover your true passion and potential. By taking responsibility for creating the kind of life you really want, you can become all that you were meant to be.

# EPILOGUE

It took me six years to write this book. During this time I have worked with countless Nice Guys and their partners. I have averaged three No More Mr. Nice Guy men's groups per week. In group time alone, that's over 1,800 hours of working with Nice Guys. During this time, I have observed many exciting and profound things.

I have watched countless men go from being helpless, passive, controlling, and resentful victims to becoming empowered, integrated males.

I have seen numerous relationships dramatically improve, and I've seen just as many die an overdue death.

I've listened to unsolicited testimonials and read letters of gratitude from both men and women about the changes they have experienced in their lives.

I have received responses from men and women all over the world who have seen themselves or someone they love in the description of the Nice Guy on my website.

Based on observing all of these things, here is my greatest discovery: The tools and insights presented in *No More Mr. Nice Guy* work.

Having finished reading this book, I encourage you to start again at the beginning. Take the time to do the Breaking Free exercises. If you have not already done so, find a safe person or group to assist you on your journey of recovery from the Nice Guy Syndrome. If you are in a relationship, ask your partner to read the book. Share with him or her the insights you are discovering about yourself.

Working the program of recovery presented in *No More Mr. Nice Guy* is one of the greatest gifts you can give yourself and your loved ones. As you learn to approve of yourself you will discover within you an unimaginable ability to love and accept love and to live life to its fullest. This kind of expansiveness is initially frightening, but it is the essence of who you are and what you are meant to be.

With this discovery of your true self comes unlimited freedom. Freedom to be just who you are. Freedom to stop seeking approval. Freedom to start getting what you want.

# NOMOREMRNICEGUY.COM

Dr. Glover offers numerous resources for recovering Nice Guys on his website: drglover.com. These include:

- Seminars, workshops, and classes
- Podcasts
- Certified coaches and therapists
- Calendar of current events

Take advantage of the resources offered on drglover.com and start getting what you want in love and life.

# SUGGESTED RESOURCES
# FOR RECOVERING NICE GUYS

### Beattie, Melody
*Codependent No More; How to Stop Controlling Others And Start Caring For Yourself,* 1987, Hazelden
Written primarily from the prospective of alcoholic family systems, this early book on codependency applies to both men and women.

### Bly, Robert
*Iron Fohn,* 1990, Addison-Wesley
Bly uses myth and poetry to focus on the ways men are wounded in modern cultures.

### Carnes, Patrick, Ph.D.
*Out of the Shadows; Understanding Sexual Addiction*
1983, CompCare Publishers
A leading expert on sexual addiction, Carnes's books cover issues of personal addiction and traumatic bonds in relationships, www.sexhelp.com.

### Eldredge, John
*Wild at Heart; Discovering The Secret Of A Man's Soul*
2001, Thomas Nelson Publishers
Eldredge explores how Christian men are conditioned to be "nice" and how this robs them of their true masculine selves, www.ransomedhearts.com.

### Farrell, Warren
*The Myth Of Male Power,* 1993, Simon & Schuster
A former president of the New York Chapter of the NOW, Farrell has written numerous books on men's issues and relationships, www.warrenfarrell.com.

**Gurian, Michael**

*The Wonder Of Boys,* 1996, Tarcher/Putman
Gurian addresses the unique qualities and characteristics of boys and adolescent males in his books, www.michaelgurian.com.

**Hastings, Anne Stirling, Ph.D.**

*America's Sexual Crisis,* 2001, Wellness Institute
Hastings' books focus on helping individuals and couples overcome their sexual wounds and the dysfunctional conditioning of society in order to experience powerful, unfolding sex, www.selfhelpbooks.com.

**Jeffers, Susan, Ph.D.**

*Feel The Fear And Do It Anyway,* 1987, Fawcett Columbine
The founder of Fear Busters, Jeffers's book is a readable and powerful prescription for facing and overcoming fear, www.susanjeffers.com.

**Meleton, Marcus Pierce, Jr.**

*Nice Guys Don't Get Laid,* 1993, Sharkbait Press
A humorous look at why Nice Guys have difficulty in their personal and sexual relationships, www.sharkbaitpress.com/niceguys.html.

**Paglia, Camille**

An historian and observer of modern culture, Paglia frequently touches on issues of personal and sexual relationship dynamics, dir. salon.com/topics/camille_paglia/index.html.

**Peck, M. Scott, M.D.**

*The Road Less Traveled,* 1978, Simon & Schuster
In one of the best selling self-help books of all time, Peck addresses issues of discipline, love, and spirituality, www.mscottpeck.com.

**Scott, Neill**

A pioneer in identifying, explaining, and treating the Nice Guy Syndrome, especially as this phenomenon pertains to single men and their relationships with women. He offers an audio tape titled, *The Nice Guy and Why He Always Fails With Women,* which can be ordered from his web site at ve.net/relationships.

# LIST OF TITLES WITH ISBN NO.

| ISBN | TITLE |
|---|---|
| 9788194914129 | 1984 |
| 9789390575220 | 1984 & Animal Farm (2In1) |
| 9789390575572 | 1984 & Animal Farm (2In1): The International Best-Selling Classics |
| 9789390575848 | 35 Sonnets |
| 9789390575329 | A Clergyman's Daughter |
| 9789390575923 | A Study In Scarlet |
| 9789390896097 | A Tale Of Two Cities |
| 9789390896837 | Abide in Christ |
| 9789390896202 | Abraham Lincoln |
| 9789390896912 | Absolute Surrender |
| 9789390896608 | African American Classic Collection |
| 9789390575305 | Aldous Huxley: The Collected Works |
| 9789390896141 | An Autobiography of M. K. Gandhi |
| 9789390575886 | Animal Farm |
| 9789390575619 | Animal Farm & The Great Gatsby (2In1) |
| 9789390575626 | Animal Farm & We |
| 9789390896158 | Anna Karenina |
| 9789390575534 | Antic Hay |
| 9789390896165 | Antony & Cleopatra |
| 9789390896172 | As I Lay Dying |
| 9789390896226 | As You like it |
| 9789390575671 | At Your Command |
| 9789390575350 | Awakened Imagination |
| 9789390575114 | Be What You Wish |
| 9789390896233 | Believe In yourself |
| 9789390896998 | Best of Charles Darwin: The Origin of Species & Autobiography |
| 9789390896684 | Best Of Horror : Dracula And Frankenstein |
| 9789390575503 | Best Of Mark Twain (The Adventures of Tom Sawyer AND The Adventures of Huckleberry Finn) |
| 9789390896769 | Black History Collection |
| 9789390575756 | Brave New World, Animal Farm & 1984 (3in1) |
| 9789390896240 | Brother Karamzov |
| 9789390575053 | Bulleh Shah Poetry |
| 9789390575725 | Burmese Days |

| | |
|---|---|
| 9789390896257 | Bushido |
| 9789390896066 | Can't Hurt Me |
| 9788194914112 | Chanakya Neeti: With The Complete Sutras |
| 9789390896042 | Crime and Punishment |
| 9789390575527 | Crome Yellow |
| 9789390575046 | Down and Out in Paris and London |
| 9789390896844 | Dracula |
| 9789390575442 | Emersons Essays: The Complete First & Second Series (Self-Reliance & Other Essays) |
| 9789390575749 | Emma |
| 9789390575817 | Essential Tozer Collection - The Pursuit of God & The Purpose of Man |
| 9789390896578 | Fascism What It Is and How to Fight It |
| 9789390575688 | Feeling is the Secret |
| 9789390575190 | Five Lessons |
| 9789390575954 | Frankenstein |
| 9789390575237 | Franz Kafka: Collected Works |
| 9789390575282 | Franz Kafka: Short Stories |
| 9789390575060 | George Orwell Collected Works |
| 9789390575077 | George Orwell Essays |
| 9789390575213 | George Orwell Poems |
| 9788194914150 | Greatest Poetry Ever Written Vol 1 |
| 9788194914143 | Greatest Poetry Ever Written Vol 1 |
| 9789390896301 | Gulliver's Travel |
| 9789390575961 | Gunaho Ka Devta |
| 9789390575893 | H. P. Lovecraft Selected Stories Vol 1 |
| 9789390575978 | H. P. Lovecraft Selected Stories Vol 2 |
| 9789390896059 | Hamlet |
| 9789390575022 | His Last Bow: Some Reminiscences of Sherlock Holmes |
| 9789390896134 | History of Western Philosophy |
| 9789390575121 | Homage To Catalonia |
| 9789390896219 | How to develop self-confidence and Improve public Speaking |
| 9789390896295 | How to enjoy your life and your Job |
| 9789390575633 | How to own your own mind |
| 9789390896318 | How to read Human Nature |
| 9789390896325 | How to sell your way through the life |
| 9789390896370 | How to use the laws of mind |
| 9789390896387 | How to use the power of prayer |

| | |
|---|---|
| 9789390896028 | How to win friends & Influence People |
| 9788194824176 | How To Win Friends and Influence People |
| 9789390896103 | Humility The Beauty of Holiness |
| 9789390896653 | Imperialism the Highest Stage of Capitalism |
| 9789390575084 | In Our Time |
| 9789390575169 | In Our Time & Three Stories and Ten poems |
| 9789390575145 | James Allen: The Collected Works |
| 9789390896189 | Jesus Himself |
| 9789390575480 | Jo's Boys |
| 9789390896394 | Julius Caesar |
| 9789390575404 | Keep the Aspidistra Flying |
| 9789390896400 | Kidnapped |
| 9789390896424 | King Lear |
| 9789390575824 | Lady Susan |
| 9789390896455 | Law of Success |
| 9789390896264 | Lincoln The Unknown |
| 9789390575565 | Little Men |
| 9789390575640 | Little Women |
| 9788194914174 | Lost Horizon |
| 9789390896462 | Macbeth |
| 9789390896929 | Man Eaters of Kumaon |
| 9789390896523 | Man The Dwelling Place of God |
| 9789390896349 | Man The Dwelling Place of God |
| 9789390575909 | Mansfield Park |
| 9788194914136 | Manto Ki 25 Sarvshreshth Kahaniya |
| 9789390896509 | Marxism, Anarchism, Communism |
| 9789390575664 | Mathematical Principles of Natural Philosophy |
| 9788194914198 | Meditations |
| 9789390575800 | Mein Kampf |
| 9789390575794 | Memory How To Develop, Train, And Use It |
| 9789390896486 | Mind Power |
| 9789390896585 | Money |
| 9789390575039 | Mortal Coils |
| 9789390575770 | My Life and Work |
| 9789390896035 | Narrative of the Life of Frederick Douglass |
| 9789390575152 | Neville Goddard: The Collected Works |
| 9789390575985 | Northanger Abbey |
| 9789390896530 | Notes From Underground |

| | |
|---|---|
| 9789390896547 | Oliver Twist |
| 9789390575459 | On War |
| 9789390575541 | One, None and a Hundred Thousand |
| 9789390896554 | Othelo |
| 9789390575435 | Out Of This World |
| 9789390575015 | Persuasion |
| 9789390575510 | Prayer The Art Of Believing |
| 9789390575091 | Pride and Prejudice |
| 9789390896561 | Psychic Perception |
| 9789390575381 | Rabindranath Tagore - 5 Best Short Stories Vol 2 |
| 9789390575367 | Rabindranath Tagore - Short Stories (Masters Collections Including The Childs Return) |
| 9789390575374 | Rabindranath Tagore 5 Best Short Stories Vol 1 (Including The Childs Return |
| 9789390896622 | Romeo & Juliet |
| 9789390896127 | Sanatana Dharma |
| 9789390575596 | Seedtime & Harvest |
| 9789390896639 | Selected Stories of Guy De Maupassant |
| 9789390575206 | Self-Reliance & Other Essays |
| 9789390575176 | Sense and Sensibility |
| 9789390575299 | Shyamchi Aai |
| 9789390896738 | Socialism Utopian and Scientific |
| 9789390896646 | Success Through a Positive Mental Attitude |
| 9789390575428 | The Adventures of Huckleberry Finn |
| 9789390575183 | The Adventures of Sherlock Holmes |
| 9789390575343 | The Adventures of Tom Sawyer |
| 9789390896691 | The Alchemy Of Happiness |
| 9789390575862 | The Art Of Public Speaking |
| 9789390896288 | The Autobiography Of Charles Darwin |
| 9788194914181 | The Best of Franz Kafka: The Metamorphosis & The Trial |
| 9789390575008 | The Call Of Cthulhu and Other Weird Tales |
| 9789390575107 | The Case-Book of Sherlock Holmes |
| 9789390896110 | The Castle Of Otranto |
| 9789390896745 | The Communist Manifesto |
| 9789390575589 | The Complete Fiction of H. P. Lovecraft |
| 9789390575497 | The Complete Works of Florence Scovel Shinn |
| 9789390896820 | The Conquest of Breard |
| 9789390896813 | The Diary of a Young Girl |

| | |
|---|---|
| 9789390896332 | The Diary of a Young Girl The Definitive Edition of the Worlds Most Famous Diary |
| 9789390575701 | The Great Gatsby, Animal Farm & 1984 (3In1) |
| 9789390575312 | The Greatest Works Of George Orwell (5 Books) Including 1984 & Non-Fiction |
| 9789390575992 | The Hound of Baskervilles |
| 9789390896707 | The Idiot |
| 9789390896714 | The Invisible Man |
| 9789390575657 | The Knowledge of the holy |
| 9789390575558 | The Law & the Promise |
| 9789390896721 | The Law Of Attraction |
| 9789390896776 | The Leader in you |
| 9789390896363 | The Life of Christ |
| 9789390896196 | The Man-Eating Leopard of Rudraprayag |
| 9789390896783 | The Master Key to Riches |
| 9789390575268 | The Memoirs Of Sherlock Holmes |
| 9789390896479 | The Midsummer Night's Dream |
| 9789390575466 | The Mill On The Floss |
| 9789390896790 | The Miracles of your mind |
| 9789390896660 | The Mutual Aid A Factor in Evolution |
| 9789390896448 | The Origin of Species |
| 9789390896905 | The Peter Kropotkin Anthology The Conquest of Bread & Mutual Aid A Factor of Evolution |
| 9789390896806 | The Picture of Dorian Gray |
| 9789390896271 | The Picture of Dorian Gray |
| 9789390575275 | The Power Of Awareness |
| 9789390896356 | The Power of Concentration |
| 9788194824169 | The Power of Positive Thinking |
| 9789390575411 | The Power of the Spoken Word |
| 9788194914105 | The Power Of Your Subconscious Mind |
| 9789390896899 | The Power of Your Subconscious Mind |
| 9789390896417 | The Principles of Communism |
| 9789390575787 | The Psychology Of Mans Possible Evolution |
| 9789390896615 | The Psychology of Salesmanship |
| 9789390575732 | The Pursuit of God |
| 9789390575398 | The Pursuit of Happiness |
| 9789390896851 | The Quick and Easy Way to effective Speaking |
| 9789390575947 | The Return Of Sherlock Holmes |

| | |
|---|---|
| 9789390575138 | The Road To Wigan Pier |
| 9789390896981 | The Root of the Righteous |
| 9789390575855 | The Science Of Being Well |
| 9788194914167 | The Science Of Getting Rich, The Science Of Being Great & The Science Of Being Well (3In1) |
| 9789390896011 | The Screwtape Letters |
| 9789390896073 | The Screwtape Letters |
| 9789390575336 | The Secret Door to Success |
| 9789390575695 | The Secret Of Imagining |
| 9789390896868 | The Secret Of Success |
| 9789390896431 | The Seven Last Words |
| 9789390575930 | The Sign of the Four |
| 9789390896004 | The Sonnets |
| 9789390896516 | The Souls of Black Folk |
| 9789390896875 | The Sound and The Fury |
| 9789390575244 | The State and Revolution |
| 9789390896882 | The Story of My Life |
| 9789390896936 | The Story Of Oriental Philosophy |
| 9789390896752 | The Strange Case of Dr. Jekyll and Mr. Hyde |
| 9789390896943 | The Tempest |
| 9789390575916 | The Valley Of Fear |
| 9789390575879 | The Wind in the willows |
| 9789390896080 | The Wind in the willows |
| 9789390575763 | Their eyes were watching gofd |
| 9789390575831 | Three Stories |
| 9789390896950 | Twelfth Night |
| 9789390896592 | Twelve Years a Slave |
| 9789390896677 | Up from Slavery |
| 9789390896974 | Value Price and Profit |
| 9789390896967 | Wake Up and Live |
| 9789390896493 | With Christ in the School of Prayer |
| 9789390575602 | Your Faith is Your Fortune |
| 9789390575473 | Your Infinite Power To Be Rich |
| 9789390575251 | Your Word is Your Wand |
| 9789390575718 | Youth |
| 9789391316099 | A Christmas Carol |
| 9789391316105 | A Doll's House |
| 9789391316501 | A Passage to India |

| | |
|---|---|
| 9789391316709 | A Portrait of the Artist as a Young Man |
| 9789391316112 | A Tale of Two Cities |
| 9789391316747 | A Tear and a Smile |
| 9789391316167 | Agnes Gray |
| 9789391316174 | Alice's Adventures in Wonderland |
| 9789391316136 | Anandamath |
| 9789391316181 | Anne Of Green Gables |
| 9789391316754 | Anthem |
| 9789391316198 | Around The World in 80 Days |
| 9789391316013 | As A Man Thinketh |
| 9789391316242 | Autobiography of a Yogi |
| 9789391316266 | Beyond Good and Evil |
| 9789391316761 | Bleak House |
| 9789391316778 | Chitra, a Play in One Act |
| 9789391316310 | David Copperfield |
| 9789391316075 | Demian |
| 9789391316785 | Dubliners |
| 9789391316051 | Favourite Tales from the Arabian Nights |
| 9789391316235 | Gitanjali |
| 9789391316068 | Gravity |
| 9789391316150 | Great Speeches of Abraham Lincoln |
| 9789391316662 | Guerilla Warfare |
| 9789391316839 | Kim |
| 9789391316822 | Mother |
| 9789391316211 | My Childhood |
| 9789391316846 | Nationalism |
| 9789391316327 | Oliver Twist |
| 9789391316853 | Pygmalion |
| 9789391316334 | Relativity: The Special and the General Theory |
| 9789391316389 | Scientific Healing Affirmation |
| 9789391316341 | Sons and Lovers |
| 9789391316587 | Tales from India |
| 9789391316372 | Tess of The D'Urbervilles |
| 9789391316396 | The Awakening and Selected Stories |
| 9789391316402 | The Bhagvad Gita |
| 9789391316303 | The Book of Enoch |
| 9789391316228 | The Canterville Ghost |
| 9789391316907 | The Dynamic Laws of Prosperity |

| | |
|---|---|
| 9789391316006 | The Great Gatsby |
| 9789391316860 | The Hungry Stones and Other Stories |
| 9789391316433 | The Idiot |
| 9789391316440 | The Importance of Being Earnest |
| 9789391316297 | The Light of Asia |
| 9789391316914 | The Madman His Parables and Poems |
| 9789391316457 | The Odyssey |
| 9789391316921 | The Picture of Dorian Gray |
| 9789391316464 | The Prince |
| 9789391316938 | The Prophet |
| 9789391316945 | The Republic |
| 9789391316518 | The Scarlet Letter |
| 9789391316143 | The Seven Laws of Teaching |
| 9789391316525 | The Story of My Experiments with Truth |
| 9789391316532 | The Tales of the Mother Goose |
| 9789391316549 | The Thirty Nine Steps |
| 9789391316594 | The Time Machine |
| 9789391316600 | The Turn of the Screw |
| 9789391316983 | The Upanishads |
| 9789391316617 | The Yellow Wallpaper |
| 9789391316426 | The Yoga Sutras of Patanjali |
| 9789391316990 | Ulysses |
| 9789391316624 | Utopia |
| 9789391316679 | Vanity Fair |
| 9789391316020 | What Is To Be Done |
| 9789391316686 | Within A Budding Grove |
| 9789391316693 | Women in Love |